Praise for

BIG GORGEOUS GOALS

"People often make the mistake of thinking that big goals are harder to accomplish than small goals. Julie Ellis shows you how to get out of the box of thinking small, so that you can imagine and realize ambitious, big gorgeous goals. I found this book personally helpful and think you will too, at whatever stage you are at in your career."
SHELLE ROSE CHARVET, author of *Words That Change Minds;* developer of the Advanced Business Influence learning program

"When everyone is saying 'think big!,' Julie Ellis is saying 'think gorgeous!' Set a goal so beautiful and outrageously bold that it blocks out the sun. In doing so, you'll learn you are capable of so much. But she doesn't sugarcoat. On the journey to gorgeous, you'll confront a lot of ugly—times when you'll doubt yourself and are tempted to think and be small. Julie provides the guide to navigate the ugly to get to gorgeous."
JENNIFER J. FONDREVAY, chief humanity officer, Day1 Ready; bestselling author of *NOW WHAT? A Survivor's Guide for Thriving Through Mergers & Acquisitions*

"I've never been a goal setter. I thought it was more important to do the hard work. Thank you, Julie Ellis, for showing us perspiration folks what investing in a little inspiration can do to change our own lives, and the lives of so many others. This book will leave you with a vision of what's possible and a plan for how to go get it."
LIANE DAVEY, *New York Times*–bestselling author of *The Good Fight*

"I thoroughly enjoyed Julie Ellis's *Big Gorgeous Goals* as an entrepreneur, a woman leader, and an executive coach. Julie takes the reader through her journey building Mabel's Labels, and she shares the enlightening experiences of other entrepreneurs in all different businesses. Julie is open and authentic about her experiences and her advice insightful. She is unafraid to share her good experiences along with the challenges. Her stories resonated with me and aligned with much of my own experiences in building a business. Entrepreneurship is always a risk; it doesn't always work. When it does, it is rewarding. I recommend this book to anyone who is thinking about building a business."

SANDRA OLIVER, founder, Impact Coaches

"Julie Ellis's must-read book is for anyone who has big goals and is looking for advice on how to make those goals come to life. Too many times we get trapped in our own heads and are unable to make things happen for ourselves. Julie's book is full of important information and support to help you attain all your big gorgeous goals!"

LAURA BERG, author of *Thriving Life: How to Live Your Best Life No Matter the Cards You're Dealt*

BIG
GORGEOUS
GOALS

JULIE ELLIS

BIG
GORGEOUS
GOALS

How Bold Women
Achieve Great Things

Some names and identifying details have been changed to
protect the privacy of individuals.

Cataloguing in publication information is available from
Library and Archives Canada.
ISBN 978-1-77458-148-3 (paperback)
ISBN 978-1-77458-149-0 (ebook)

Page Two
pagetwo.com

Edited by Kendra Ward
Copyedited by Steph VanderMeulen
Proofread by Alison Strobel
Cover and interior design by Jennifer Lum
Printed and bound in Canada by Friesens
Distributed in Canada by Raincoast Books
Distributed in the US and internationally by Macmillan

22 23 24 25 26   5 4 3 2 1

biggorgeousgoals.com

For Christy, an original big goal-getter.
The world isn't the same without you.

Contents

Introduction *1*
The Power of Embracing Big Gorgeous Goals

1 The Box *9*
How to Break Out When You're Trapped in Small Thinking

2 Big Thinking *23*
How to Be Bold

3 Big Gorgeous Goals *39*
What Happens When You Reach for the Stars

4 The Inflection Point *51*
How to Sense Into and Navigate Change

5 Founder as Leader *63*
How to Be the Boss of a Stellar Workplace

6 Wise Counsel *77*
How to Invest in Yourself

7 The Numbers Game *91*
What You Need to Know to Profit

8 The Choices *103*
How to Make Big Decisions

9 Caring for Yourself *117*
How to Survive the Roller Coaster

Conclusion *131*
A Bigger Yes

Acknowledgments *143*

Notes *145*

INTRODUCTION

The Power of Embracing
Big Gorgeous Goals

AS HIGH-ACHIEVING WOMEN leaders and entrepreneurs, we know that we should be thinking expansively about our businesses. That we should set big goals. And I believe that we all want to do that—but something gets in our way. Why do some women have such success in realizing their big dreams and goals? They seem to be so far beyond conventional limitations, leaving the rest of us in the dust of our to-do lists.

This book is about how to set big gorgeous goals, the ones so big that they block out the sun, the ones that scare you; they keep you up at night because you fear they are beyond your grasp. These goals are very different from the safe, achievable goals you know you can accomplish because they feel tidy and contained. Your big gorgeous goals have the power to move you out of a state of "stuckness" when you've plateaued, propelling your life and career to the next level.

Starting a business is a big gorgeous goal for a lot of people. You have an idea; you know you want the freedom to be your own boss. Then how do you take the leap of faith required to do it? Your goal may be related to breaking into a new market, scaling up your business, launching a new product, or even starting a new endeavor after reaching the entrepreneurial dream of selling your business, like I did. For some, a big gorgeous goal might be about what to do when you aren't working or are in retirement—it is a choice about how you want to *live*.

What does the goal you want to set look like? For me, writing this book was a big gorgeous goal! I have never been a writer. I'm a coach, and as I was developing workshops and doing speaking engagements, I realized that adding a book to my offerings would be beneficial. At times, it felt overwhelming. But I persevered, and here I am. Well before that, at the beginning of my career, setting a big gorgeous goal prompted me to leave my day job and find the life I wanted.

At the time, I was working as a financial planner. Growing up, I hadn't imagined a job in that field, but after I finished school, it was a "steady paycheck and benefits" for my young family while the man who became my husband set up a business. Life was stable, but it didn't feel particularly exciting to me. I achieved everything on my to-do list, doing the expected— but I definitely did not reach for the stars with my thinking!

Then a dream started to form. Some friends from university and I all had young children and we had similarly encountered a logistical problem: When we sent our children to day care, we were told to label everything they brought with them. The day care center didn't have a labeling solution for us, and we decided we could do better than using permanent marker and masking tape. Thus, in a basement in Hamilton, Ontario, Canada, we began a business creating customized labels for children's clothes and belongings that would grow beyond our wildest imaginings. Two basements and a commercial space (which we also expanded) later, our company, Mabel's Labels, employed a team of forty people and had eight-figure sales. Mabel's was a social media powerhouse with an amazing celebrity following. It sold products into Walmart and Target. Then, after thirteen years in business, my cofounders and I decided to sell to a large publicly traded company that owned the Avery Labels brand.

A new journey began for me, and it wasn't what you might expect. After we sold the business, I had no idea how to move forward. I had reached a pinnacle, and a (totally normal) plateau followed, but having arrived there, I had no idea what to do. I ended up in a downward spiral, and not until I set a big gorgeous goal to launch my coaching business did I start to climb again.

Outward and Upward

What allows certain women to keep reaching outward, upward, successively moving to the next level? While writing and researching this book, I spoke to nearly twenty women from different backgrounds. Some of them are corporate leaders who are entrepreneurial in their navigation of the corporate ladder. Some are entrepreneurs, across a variety of businesses and industries. Some have backgrounds in the military, where they carved out new paths for women as they rose in the ranks. Listening to each of these women speak about how they set big goals and chased wild dreams, I realized that although they all followed disparate paths, their routes shared common elements. Women who set big gorgeous goals and achieve them find systems to reach their dreams. They achieve the unexpected not through perfection or by always winning but by picking themselves up after setbacks and failure, dusting off, and getting back at it. Rather than giving in to overwhelm, they figure out the path to realizing big gorgeous goals.

And you can too.

Possibilities open up when you set big goals, it's true; yet what surprises me is the underpinning of the biggest aspirations—the massive amounts of mettle you need to bring your goals alive.

Think of an iceberg. Only 10 percent of it sits above water, while the other 90 percent exists beneath the water's surface. A big gorgeous goal is the same: only 10 percent of it is about dreaming up the goal and shouting it out to the world, while the other 90 percent is the work of accomplishing it. We often see and admire the extraordinary 10 percent in others without accounting for the hard work, grit, and determination it took to get there. The 90 percent of reaching a goal includes:

- chunking it out

- finding a cadence between the practical and tactical steps toward it

- checking in to measure progress

- making decisions

- delegating wisely

- bulldogging high-performing teams

In the pages ahead, we'll keep returning to this 10/90 metaphor. As you consider how to achieve your entrepreneurial dreams, I offer you the 10 percent—the blue-sky concepts that will keep propelling you toward your goal. A 90 percent section digs deeper, giving you the how-to—the work of achieving a goal that often gets forgotten. I also include stories from my own entrepreneurial career, and those of the women I interviewed, to inspire you to step out and set your own big gorgeous goals.

Keep Reaching

As I write this, we are well into a global pandemic. Keeping up with the chores, educating children from home, and leaving the workforce in droves, women have been set back further during the last couple of years than they have been in decades. Yet, these changes give us all an opportunity to pause and consider what we really want. There is no more important time than right now for us to set big gorgeous goals, and to strive to achieve them.

Maybe you feel like you've hit a rut. A big gorgeous goal will release you from it; it will allow you to soar. Being afraid or feeling overwhelmed by the sheer enormity of your dream is no excuse. What if you reach for the stars, and at the very least you land on the moon? What if you break out of the box you contain yourself in, expand your thinking, and stand in the confidence that you can change the trajectory of your life, maybe even of the world?

1

THE BOX

How to Break Out When You're Trapped in Small Thinking

box

/bäks/   *noun*

a container with a flat base and sides, typically square or rectangular and having a lid

N 2003, AFTER spending a year testing and researching how we could make a cute, durable label, my three business partners and I started Mabel's Labels. We each had young children in day care and school, and we wanted to apply the labels to our kids' belongings when we shuttled them out into the world. We didn't like the idea of labeling with masking tape and a permanent marker. A simple desire initiated our quest for a better way to label everything!

When we launched, we set a small budget for stamps and wrote a letter to announce our new business. Unfortunately, we had more friends to send the letter to than we had money for stamps! But as we folded the letters and addressed and stamped the envelopes, we popped a bottle of champagne and imagined that Mabel's would have an IPO someday.

This little business worked its way through two basement offices in my sister-in-law's homes. When we outgrew the first office, we decided that she should buy a bigger house, with a bigger basement. (It made sense to us at the time!) From that second basement, we moved to a commercial space where we could grow and take on more square footage as we needed it.

We had great fun decorating the office of our new commercial space so that it reflected the lively, collaborative, unique culture we were creating for our business and our team. Painting and furnishing the office was a labor filled with love and excitement! We even decorated the walls with some Mabel's art prints and poster-sized copies of ads we had placed. We also adorned those walls with quotes that inspired us. There were at least a couple dozen of them placed throughout the office. Of all the sayings we posted to those walls, my favorite was "World domination is a full-time job."

This became my mantra. It kept me going during tough times, when it felt like I would never learn what I needed to; when I thought I would never get things right. This quote inspired me to pick myself up off the floor and look at the big picture. To think big. To dream about what supposedly couldn't be done. To make the impossible possible. It animated a lot of ideas that others thought were crazy! Start a new, full-color line of labels? "The printing technology isn't ready," some said. "Organize a fundraising program to allow organizations to reach their financial goals? How could you possibly administrate that?" others chimed in. "Sell into a national chain by fall? It can't be done!" But reaching into the unknown for what magic lay there never felt tired—it always felt fun.

After thirteen years in the label-making trenches, we had reached eight-figure sales and had around forty employees. We had built an award-winning, market-leading brand that was well known in the children's label market. We had developed a direct-to-consumer business that was thriving, and we had launched a retail division, selling labels into Walmart and Target. We had inspired dozens of other businesses in the segment we carved out for ourselves. We had a celebrity following and a large social media presence.

Then Avery Labels came calling.

In a whirlwind, filled with excitement and pressure to get things right, we did rigorous due diligence and completed the sale of our beloved business at the end of 2015. I planned to stay on for a long-term relationship with the new owners, although I wasn't sure exactly how I would feel when I was no longer the business's owner. During the sale, I had taken on a ton of work, which meant I avoided having to think about it.

I woke up filled with anticipation and trepidation on the first business day of 2016. That morning, we would be announcing to our team that we had sold the business, and immediately thereafter, the new owners would join us so that the team could hear from them directly. The team's reaction? They were thrilled for us. And a new era for Mabel's Labels began.

Over the next few months, the changes came fast and furious. Avery wanted to leverage their strengths in the printing industry and impart their knowledge about how Mabel's could do things better. All amazing stuff. But change management felt like a fire hose turned on us! Integrating a tiny enterprise like Mabel's into such a large infrastructure was quite a project. The reporting requirements of a publicly traded company left us breathless.

During those first weeks and months, I began to feel disconnected from the parts of the business that I had most enjoyed: setting strategy, and creating a plan and rallying the team around it. As I moved into a different kind of leadership role, I felt less satisfied. After wrestling with the decision for months, I chose to leave the business. I decided pretty quickly, considering my thirteen-year history at Mabel's.

And the move upended my life.

On June 30, six months after the acquisition, I was out in the world, with open space in front of me and no real plans to fill it. I was more than a little excited. Right away, I went on vacation with my family, and summer settled in. I reset, rested, and recovered. My husband and I stayed at our cottage, traveled on weekends, and spent more time with our kids. It was a glorious summer.

But as fall arrived and our routine turned to school and work, I began sitting on the couch—a lot. So often, in fact, that couch-vigil became my new normal. The race to the sale had been long and labor intensive, so resting was definitely still on the agenda. But as quiet weeks turned into months that slipped by, I contemplated what to do next, and I found myself frozen.

In truth, I had once imagined myself with an office at Mabel's Labels for the rest of my life. I had planned to go there every day, even in retirement, to drink coffee, read the paper, and check in on the state of the business. Until I was out in the world, it had never occurred to me that my future would look different.

Suddenly, the friends I had seen every day for more than a decade were too busy to connect as they continued the work of business building. Finding myself destabilized and quite alone, I questioned my success. Would I always identify as the cofounder of an amazing Canadian success story? Was it all just a little bit of luck?

I sank further into my living room couch. It was a comfortable place, after all. I tried to imagine raising myself up off the couch, but it seemed to me that the seat cushion was stuck to my butt!

It sounds ridiculous, but figuratively, that's how things were for me. Accomplishing anything with a couch cushion stuck to your butt is nearly impossible. For six months, I languished on that metaphorical couch, the voices in my head telling me that I wasn't good enough, hadn't been successful enough, and the best parts of my career were in the rearview mirror.

Looking back, I can see that this time was not a total loss. I formed a new brand for myself, hired someone to create a logo, and worked with a coach to develop programs for entrepreneurs. I was laying track for the next stage of my life and career. I was beginning to think about how I could use my creativity to do big things and bring my message to lots of people. But I lacked the motivation to genuinely start. And so, I lived in a sort of inertia for many months.

I tried my hand at consulting and acquired a few clients. Despite the good work, I struggled to find the right clients, who could afford me, and to secure meaningful work. I lacked confidence that I was qualified to do the work. When one of my clients said she wanted me for my expertise, I thought, *Do you know how inexperienced I am?* My self-doubts were crushing me. Even as I built a new business, I was placing myself in a box that limited my potential and kept me small when I needed to once again think big.

The 10 Percent: Think "World Domination"

You've likely heard of thinking outside the box. The expression means to explore ideas outside the norm, to be unlimited—world domination big!—in your thinking. At Mabel's Labels, we did this by dreaming up new products that hadn't been in the market before. We experimented, tried new things, and carved our own path forward. We got used to people telling us that it couldn't be done and not listening to them. We made world domination our full-time job. Now, I apply that same thinking to my work as a coach and encourage my clients to do the same.

Thinking in terms of "world domination" means not giving in to limiting thoughts, or to the constant demands of your daily to-do list. It means embracing an ethos of possibility, making time every day for big-picture thinking, and learning to trust that even when the future or outcomes are murky, you are initiating a process to realize your big gorgeous goals—those goals so big that they block out the sun. Something opens up when you think in these terms. You spark creativity and untether yourself from expectations. You allow for expansive, strategic, blue-sky thoughts to take up space.

The 90 Percent: Overcome Thinking Small

When you set out to achieve something big, you are at a place of opportunity—unless sabotaging voices in your head take control. Self-sabotaging thoughts that tell you to stay small are often at their most potent when you're making your first moves toward a big goal. And as my story above demonstrates, sometimes those voices are strongest after a huge success, when you're on a plateau and preparing to start another climb.

During those initial months of my post-Mabel's life, I felt I had achieved something great, but eventually I began to feel trapped inside a box that was shrinking around me. The voices in my head were strong, and I was vulnerable. Big dreams seemed light-years away. World domination was a faint memory. At the time, I couldn't even see what was happening to me. Escaping the box was out of the question. I'm not sure I could have even opened the lid to stick my head out and look around.

When you reach a pinnacle, you often then hit a plateau. For any number of reasons, you get stuck, inertia sets in, and staying in this spot becomes all too easy, cozy; you might even become complacent. But this is not a viable long-term option. The cost is too high. When I was nestled in that box, something in me knew I needed to start seeking out the clients I deserved, to believe in my own abilities. I needed to change the tune that was playing inside my head and start believing in myself again.

I needed to think big.

Don't Play Small

People get stuck for many reasons. Understanding why and how you are stuck and how small that makes your world can be difficult. But if you can grasp the "why," you can change things for the future by being aware of how to avoid your own pitfalls.

Objectively assessing your own progress is never easy! But you can start by taking a good look at where you are now. We all put ourselves in boxes—what does yours look like?

The big change of selling my business thrust me into a different arena, where I struggled to find my footing. Have you gone through a big change that has thrown off your game? Perhaps you grew your business and invested in adding a team under you. This changes your job on a daily basis. Suddenly, you have many unscheduled hours in your calendar to work *on* your business. It can feel intimidating, a little scary even. A big change can happen so quietly that you may not even notice until you are trapped in much smaller than usual habits of thinking and doing.

For me to get out of the box I found myself in, I needed to reignite belief in myself. I had to rediscover my desire to take risks. I did this by taking time to visualize what success would look like. What needed to happen to tell me I was on the right path? Once I could see where I was going, I then needed to connect to this vision regularly. At first, I reminded myself of it every single day. Then, I needed to figure out how to take the necessary steps forward so that I could start realizing the vision. Some days, this was hard. I didn't progress at all. I also needed to be kind to myself as I gingerly stepped into big-thinking mode once again. I reminded myself that we all take two steps forward and then slide back a little. That's just part of the process, not something to be discouraged about.

Others usually see you with an objectivity you lack when examining yourself. Hearing from trusted people about where they think you're playing small is important, as is seeking honest feedback regularly and in a targeted, productive way. Who do you trust to give you the support you need as you birth something new? Which of your people most believe in you and want to see you succeed? Who has the courage to help you hone your ideas, to improve them in ways you couldn't imagine on your own? Figure out who are your trusted sounding boards—people who give you real advice and don't just tell you what you want to hear. Ask for targeted feedback by using specific questions so you get the precise kind of feedback you need to break out of your box. You might ask:

- What are my strengths?

- I'm thinking of doing this next . . . What do you think?

- How can I progress faster?

- What options am I missing?

- How can I overcome this obstacle?

These might have helped me get off that couch faster. Of course, it's not just about asking the questions, but also about finding a way to believe in yourself again so that you can begin to move forward.

Avoid the Checklist Manifesto

Making time for big thinking is important—so much so that you need to schedule it in your calendar. Otherwise, without even realizing it, you may get caught in the day-to-day. If you create a giant to-do list and then set about crossing many things off it, you may in fact simply be avoiding a look at a wider view. When you are stuck in a place that feels small, you may lose sight of the big picture in favor of execution mode. This is a trap laid by fears! You keep yourself busy and "productive," but you can't see the blue-sky goals you need for long-term progress.

Kelsey Ramsden is a serial entrepreneur who has built multiple businesses from the ground up—including a construction business that built highways, airports, and other big infrastructure, as well as a company that offered subscription boxes for parents and kids. Currently the CEO of MINDCURE, a medical mental wellness company, she was named Canada's Female Entrepreneur of the Year in 2012 and 2013. In discussing how to break free of the limitations we place on ourselves, Kelsey said, "I think a lot of people wind up playing small and choosing to get stuck in that checklist manifesto. The idea is that, well, if I just do these eight things, I'm not going to have to look at the bigger picture of what's happening here. So I will stay in this little echo chamber of execution."

Can you afford yourself the grace and space of time to figure things out, to alleviate the pressure that closes you up in that small box? Big changes present the perfect opportunity to let yourself be expansive. To think outside the box. To dream and wish for new things.

Starting Something Big

When you achieve something great and then hit a plateau, moving forward may feel scary. This fear may keep you small; you've done something wonderful, but now you feel like you have something to outdo.

Author and entrepreneur Paula S. White spent years building sales teams in the veterinary and medical distribution fields. Then she created Side B Consulting, an innovative coaching company that mentors leaders through music to help them shift their perspective on leadership. Paula and I discussed what happens when you've done something big and set out anew to achieve a big gorgeous goal. She said, "You get pushed into the pool again and must either sink or swim. Sometimes I think that when we dream big, we forget about the little steps that you need to take to get there. You start to wonder, *Why aren't we there yet?* It's also about having the patience to let that dream unfold."

Likewise, Julie Kenney spoke of the time it can take to develop something new. For a few years, Julie could see a change in her business coming. She knew that her company, Jewels and Pinstripes, which created gift bags for celebrity events and occasions, wasn't going to be sustainable. The bags had become commoditized, with profit margins shrinking and demand slowing. As CEO, Julie was exploring a lot of opportunities but didn't yet have a clear vision about her direction. Then, the COVID-19 pandemic hit. So, she decided to consult trusted people and to narrow down her moves to the best opportunities, while giving herself some space to refresh her vision. "I decided that I had to give myself some grace, because things were really changing, especially during the pandemic,"

Julie said. "I knew that something would come eventually—I just needed to be patient. It was exactly like planting seeds. It's hard being patient waiting for them to grow." Deciding not to keep all the plates spinning takes courage. Julie committed to shifting the business and creating new doors to open.

If you get stuck in small thinking, know that you are in a process—and that it's time to reset and get back on the path of setting those big gorgeous goals! The tools in the pages ahead will help you navigate changes and ensure that you break out of that small box and keep thinking big for yourself.

BIG GORGEOUS TAKEAWAYS

- Even a huge success can be destabilizing.

- You may need to (re)learn how to think expansively. This will ignite your movement.

- Thinking big requires self-reflection, input from trusted peers, and exercising your imagination.

- Although you need to execute day-to-day tasks, getting stuck on your checklist can impede big-picture thinking when you need it.

- Small steps and grace time are important during transition.

2

BIG THINKING

How to Be Bold

big

/big/ *adjective*

1. of considerable size, extent, or intensity
2. of considerable importance or seriousness

ONE OF OUR wildest ideas at Mabel's Labels was born of a frequent request from moms: "I have a kid going to school [or camp or day care] tomorrow, and I need labels—today!" Even with next-day shipping, we could not deliver the labels on time. This was definitely one of the downsides of having a mail-order business. Despite providing world-class customer service, we would always be at the mercy of delivery agents. And so, a big goal was born—to make a cute, durable label that could be sold at retail outlets like Target and could be personalized on the fly.

That felt like a lofty goal. Up to this point, we had been printing custom labels in our own factory, located inside our offices in Hamilton, Ontario, Canada. We had developed processes, procedures, and our own in-house-built software, and we efficiently created labels that were pretty much indestructible. But to sell into big retailers, we would need to have labels mass produced.

First, we had some serious arts and crafts to do. We needed a prototype to show our suppliers how we envisioned the labels working. History had taught us that our ideas often pushed suppliers into new territory, and we were always careful to be as clear as possible with them. So, off we went to create hand-made prototypes. Then, we would investigate production.

With our prototypes in hand, we attended printing trade shows and showed our samples around, looking for someone who could make them. We worked our way through our list of suppliers to see if they could introduce us to anyone who could produce our labels, and we spent a ton of time investigating the options online. We finally concluded that our labels could not be made in North America. All our experts told us to look at factories in China.

This was a huge step away from what we knew so well. One of my cofounders had a background in the printing business, and another had learned a ton about printing while running our factory. Over the years, we had built a solid network of experts that we relied on. We felt certain that we had the fundamentals to get this project done. But going overseas to make labels, across many time zones, and with a language barrier? This felt more than a little intimidating. We decided not to focus on those fears. Instead, we drafted a project plan. Step one: select factories to make samples.

A few months later, we had our first samples in hand. Then, with a great connection and a wee bit of luck, we landed a meeting at Walmart Canada to talk about placement in their back-to-school setup. On a snowy January day, full of adrenaline and hope, we told the buyers our story: we were moms who started a business in the basement, developed a celebrity following, and became a social media powerhouse. They, in turn, told us that back-to-school was already closed. They weren't sure how they would fit us in. We left the meeting a little deflated. And then we bided our time.

After a week (that felt like forever), we finally got the call: "We want to put you in our back-to-school area. And we want to include you all year in our stationery department."

We hung up the phone and did a happy dance. This news was all we had hoped for! But gradually our dance moves slowed. Then, they came to a full stop. To sell products into Walmart, we were going to need much more than our samples. We needed finished products. And we needed to deliver them in less than six months! We knew we had a ton of work to do to make this happen, and we weren't even sure how to get started.

Another terrifying prospect: The cost of being unable to deliver on this date was huge—Walmart was well known for charging penalties if you didn't deliver on time. Worse, if we didn't meet the deadline, we would miss the back-to-school window and be stuck with an enormous number of labels, with no chance of selling them and the risk of a hit to our reputation. We *had* to deliver those labels on time.

So, what did we do? Instead of giving into the fears, we dreamed bigger. We referred back to our project plan and jumped on the task list. We reviewed, revised, and built out our plan, and realized that we needed to visit the factories that had provided us the samples, in the hope that one of them would be the right fit to partner with us. We booked flights, got visas, and hopped on a plane—all within a few weeks.

By the end of February, one of my business partners and I were on the ground in China. We didn't know the language, we didn't know where we were going, and we had no idea if we would find a factory that could fill our order. But we kept putting one foot in front of the other, purposefully remaining confident that we would get the job done.

After several mishaps and touring multiple different options, we found a factory we were happy to work with. We used the company of a Canadian we had befriended on our trip to do quality control and assurance. We shipped the labels across the water, then across our vast country. We packed them up and prepared them for the back-to-school season. Most importantly, we delivered the product to Walmart on time.

Over the next couple of years, we grew that business to a million dollars in revenue. The journey had its ups and downs, but I am immensely proud of the work we did on that product line. Even years later, cruising the stationery section at Walmart Canada and seeing the labels there pleases me.

The 10 Percent: Be Bold

Looking back, I can see that so many things could have gone wrong. We were making a new product, on a scale we had not yet tackled, in a country entirely foreign to us, and with a factory we had no history with. But we had dreamed up a bold goal. It inspired us. And we pushed hard to make it happen. We *had* to make it work. So, we figured it out, and we accepted help along the way. We used our network to gain introductions, which led to more connections than we could have imagined. We cast a wide net. And when we heard a "no," we asked, "Why not?"

We had a big gorgeous goal. This is the kind of goal that's so big, it can scare the pants off you, but once you dream it up, you know you *must* make it happen. When you have such a goal, it can be helpful to remember: world domination is a full-time job. Sometimes, you may need to tell yourself that every few minutes! As we did, you may experience some luck along the way, but there will be tons of hard work too, and it may come with a difficult learning curve. So, adopt a bold mindset that you will do it, no matter what, and then learn to distinguish between what will take you there and what gets in the way.

Because here's what I know today. There are two kinds of goals:

1 **To-do list goals.** You do these and then scratch them off the list. They are often outlined as SMART or the like, so that they can be easily measured. They regularly appear on performance review forms. They make logical sense.

2 **Big gorgeous goals.** Going after these goals feels like reaching for the stars. People may tell you achieving them is not possible. These goals are exhilarating and often irrational.

Pursuing a big gorgeous goal will propel you to the next level—of your business or your life. Ask yourself: "So what if I reach for the stars and get only halfway there? What happens then? If I land on the moon instead, what would that be like?"

The 90 Percent: Create Space for the Magic

We sometimes struggle to set big gorgeous goals because we are tied up in the mundane. Ticking items off a list can be so satisfying and motivating. But those little chicken scratches can perpetually entice us into small thinking. We prioritize the treadmill of managing our inboxes and to-do lists, feeling comfortable in that safe space. But if we stay there too long, we forget about the thrill of the unknown.

Think about the unknown for a moment. What holds you back from going toward it? Fear is a major factor, and with it comes resistance. Once resistance is in play, you may feel really stuck.

Now, I know that constantly living in the unknown can be stressful and tiring. Continually surfing a learning curve, which you will always feel like you're doing when you're building a business, is incredibly difficult. You feel off-balance; you never know what will come next. But instead of allowing this to erode your confidence, you need to lean in to it, experimenting with different ways your goal can turn out and continuing on a growth path. You've got to learn to say no and to get out of the weeds.

Learn the Strategic No

Let's talk about saying no. We say no all the time: "No, I'm not ready for/No, I'm not good enough for/No, I don't know how to do that..." and on and on. We say no because our fears hold us back from achieving our true worth. Saying no in this way is inadvertently saying yes to things that fill your time and calendar (and inboxes too) but don't move you closer to your goal.

Or perhaps you default to saying yes? We all like to be a part of things; we like to say yes! Helping others, staying connected, and filling our schedules with our essential activities feels so good. And we are really busy people. It has become a societal norm to brag about how busy we keep ourselves. In fact, we're so busy that we often don't get to the important work. We might even lean on our busyness as an excuse to avoid moving on our big gorgeous goals.

You need to say no in order to focus on the work that truly grows you. Because—make no mistake—your big gorgeous goals require white space on your calendar (and in your brain). You need time to think. Time to reflect and dream. To create this space, you need to strategically say no. You can do this kindly, of course. And with the knowledge that your time is a finite commodity.

But especially when you're growing your business, saying no can be difficult. You want to seize every opportunity. But the reality is that you need to take on fewer projects and do them well—so well that they become prime examples of how to do things.

One of our challenges at Mabel's Labels was in how to choose the winning horses. We always felt as if we had more opportunities than we could take on, and we lamented it. We hashed and rehashed the options. In fact, we started the business with just one type of label. Then we added options for more shapes, colors, pictures, and fonts. We saw an endless range of products that we could create and personalize so that, with more choice to meet their tastes and needs, parents' lives would be easier. When we launched our full-color labels, moving away from the single colors with white print that had been our offering until then, it opened up many possibilities for adding on. Carving an achievable path was important to us. We wanted each project to be ambitious and something we knew we could succeed at. Over time, we realized that if we chose fewer projects and did them with excellence, good things happened. That product launch? Execution was great, product quality was high, production processes were in place. We could sell it and *win*! And so we did.

Watch for the Weeds

We value our concrete output—the work we can track and point to as our successes. In reality, "researching" online when you should be writing or filming or dreaming of what's next, or replying to five hundred emails instead of doing the creative work that will propel your business forward, is short-sighted and dangerous. Such activities distract you from the big thinking you need to do to reach for those stars and block out the sun.

How many of your daily tasks are extraneous and unimportant? Lots, I imagine. We all get caught in the weeds. This is where you mistakenly feel massively productive. You are crushing your long list of tasks, plus your inbox is empty and your filing is up to date. But your constant motion doing low-level tasks has prevented you from opening up your thinking. I myself am guilty of this. There's nothing I like more than tidy paperwork and an empty inbox. Completing these tasks can be so much easier than planning or reflecting. But at what expense? What gets in the way of saying yes to big thinking? A lack of confidence? Creative blocks? These are joy stealers and energy leakers.

Remember Kelsey Ramsden, the CEO of MINDCURE? Her strategy is to envision the future and then live as if it has already come true. Clarity isn't necessary. The trajectory and progress at a very high level take precedence over checking the boxes. For her, big thinking means to dream up a big goal and search for how it has been done before. If it hasn't been done, she figures out how to do it. Every morning, she creates a list of things she needs to check off—but she makes sure each item pertains to her big goal. She gets that quick and safe feeling that progress is being made.

In our interview, Kelsey pointed out that her big thinking isn't always right—sometimes her ideas come too soon. In 2012, she devised a subscription box for kids: subscribers received a themed monthly kit with activities and learning tools, delivered to their door. By the early 2020s, that looked like a pretty good idea, but a decade earlier, the world wasn't ready for it. Kelsey told me that when she started the business, she thought, "*This is so obvious. Everybody is busy. They all want things delivered. They want to hang with their kids, take a picture, and share it with their friends.* And I was just too soon."

But for Kelsey, being ahead of the curve only reaffirmed her dreams. Her work on the play kit set her up for her next big gorgeous goal—becoming a keynote speaker and bestselling author. All keeping her on the path of big thinking.

Thinking Big

Big thinking is about creating unique paths that are not necessarily conventional. Author and entrepreneur Fotini Iconomopoulos is a negotiation expert. In her own words, she "helps people get what they want." After working her way up in the corporate world, she took a leap and founded Forward Focusing, where she gives expert advice on commercial strategy and negotiation for large and small companies. Her book *Say Less, Get More* was published in April 2021.

Fotini habitually says yes to opportunities that seem out of the box while always keeping herself open and her eye on the next steps. She stretches the rules and often finds herself doing things that she "shouldn't" be qualified for. She said,

Although I never said, "I'm going to be the CEO someday," I just knew I was going to be successful. With that lens, I have looked for the next logical step to being successful. As opposed to "here's the direct path to my big goal..." I have consciously and subconsciously kept myself open to opportunities.

I applied to this difficult-to-get-into arts and science program at McMaster University that awards both degrees at the same time. They only let sixty people in each year, and I decided I was going to be one of them. And I did get into the program, and I hated it. So I started consulting career counselors, and they all told me the same thing:

you may perform like an ArtsSci student, but you are really well suited for business.

Coming from a family that ran a business, Fotini wanted nothing more than to go in a different direction. She wanted a corporate career as opposed to what she knew about small business. But deciding to follow the advice of the counselors, she applied to business school and was accepted into the prestigious Schulich School of Business MBA program.

"I wasn't supposed to apply, because I didn't have the required two years' [post-undergraduate] work experience," Fotini said. "But I applied anyway... After I finished, I landed a job at L'Oréal. They typically hired for marketing roles, but instead, the leadership thought, *Hmmm, you might be right for sales.* And they placed me in a unique role they didn't usually recruit MBAs for."

Fotini took an unorthodox path to becoming a sought-after consultant, speaker, and author. Her willingness to say yes and stretch herself has helped her develop a strong network and be unafraid to shift her direction.

GG Benitez, CEO and founder of industry-leading PR firm GG Benitez & Associates Public Relations, truly started at the bottom and set out on a path to change her story. At a young age, she left a bad marriage and proceeded to ascend the corporate world, then founded her own businesses, with big thinking propelling her forward moves. GG said:

I was single at twenty-two years old, with a two-year-old. In those first years on my own, I was broke, but I knew it would be temporary because the most powerful things a woman can have are freedom and education. When those things are combined, for somebody who does not take that for granted, I knew that I was going to be successful... I had my degree and I live in the United States of America. I didn't have to stay in a miserable marriage, have my spirit crushed, and be held down any longer. Then it was one step in front of the other to get those two years in. By the end of those two years, I was making great money working for this huge pharmaceutical company based on my ability to establish rapport with people and being able to communicate and articulate the benefits of the company's offerings and make money for them. So I started thinking bigger, knowing that I was good at it. It gave me the things I needed at that time: a base salary, 401(k) retirement plan, stock options, car payments, and so on. Because of that job, I was able to give my daughter the American life I dreamed of. We traveled together, learned to ski, moved to a great area. She went to great schools. That was very empowering for me.

After being very successful for seven years, I realized that I wanted to take my talents, my expertise, my intellect, and do it for myself. I began to delve into different businesses, failed. Started something else. Failed at that. Then I started something that led me to where I am now, in public relations.

GG cofounded a clothing line that she sold into Nordstrom and Bloomingdale's, although profit and sustainable income were still elusive. So she used her sales ability and engaged celebrities and media to secure attention that helped grow the brand. "And even though we had great sales and media attention," GG said, "it was hard to make money at our business. I was facing the facts that I might need to go back to pharmaceutical sales, and I wasn't at all interested in doing it."

One day, GG got a call from a buyer. She asked the caller who did their PR and learned she was looking for someone. GG said:

> I told her what I had done for my own brand and she booked me to come and present at the board meeting the following week, where they would be making the decision.
>
> The next few days were a blur. I needed to register a business, build a simple website, and read everything I could about PR. I enlisted someone who would mentor me and help me through the process of doing the work for this client—if I was able to land them. I walked into the board meeting, and I nailed it. I took that brand from performing at local malls to performing at celebrity birthday parties and being written up in *People* magazine. After that, every few months I landed another client. It just grew from there.

GG is incredibly proud of being able to lift up herself and her family with her business. And she has had many happy clients, and done events with the likes of Shonda Rhimes! Her clients are delighted with the media coverage that GG's hustle has given them. (Full disclosure: she was the PR person for Mabel's Labels when I was a co-owner there!)

BIG GORGEOUS TAKEAWAYS

- Big thinking means being bold, ignoring the naysayers who tell you "it can't be done."

- To-do list goals feel easy and safe. Big gorgeous goals may feel terrifying.

- If you reach for the stars and you land on the moon, you'll have done something incredible.

- Creating space for big thinking requires saying no to the little things and saying yes to reflection, dreaming, and planning.

3

BIG GORGEOUS GOALS

What Happens When You Reach for the Stars

goal

/gōl/ *noun*

the object of a person's ambition or effort; an aim or
desired result

SELLING MABEL'S LABELS was the realization of a big gorgeous goal thirteen years in the making. People often tell me how lucky I was to have had a business so successful that I could sell it. This comment always makes me stop and think, *What was lucky about that?*

We certainly had the luck of timing. When we started our business, no one else in North America was making customized labels for kids. We set out to build a brand that would be known and would endure, to create a product that we could stand by, with a money-back guarantee and no questions asked. Being first to market with our product gave us a leg up on the competition that quickly followed us. It also meant that we did the difficult and time-consuming work of figuring out how we were going produce the product, and what equipment was available to us. That took us more than a year! But we did just that, and our product sold because of the moms, who quickly spread the word among each other about the goods they adore.

So, really, after the luck of timing, our "luck" came with a lot of hard work, standing by our product, and making sure that it really did what we said it did. Our business also wasn't the overnight success that it appeared to be in the moment we sold it. We had put in thirteen years of hard work to make it what it was!

At the heart of it, every woman I spoke to in writing this book had the courage, big thinking, and fortitude to go after big gorgeous goals. They found the ways to get out of their boxes and set huge goals for themselves. Sometimes, they didn't even realize how big the goal was until they had the time and distance to see it. And when the path and the goal changed, they were able to pivot to move forward and continue to think big.

The 10 Percent: Reach for the Stars

In the previous chapter, I encouraged you to ask yourself, "What if I reach for the stars and don't quite make it?" You might land on the moon. Isn't that so much further ahead than where any safe, box-checking goal could get you? Being audacious and imagining the biggest goal you can is part of the process. If you feel as if you have no business setting such a big goal, you are probably on the right track.

When it comes to leadership qualities, women appear to be stronger than men in most areas, including in resilience, initiative, driving results, and developing others, to name a few. So why are we afraid to make bold choices and big goals? What can change if we seize the opportunity and set a big gorgeous goal?

Even if you don't reach it in the end, pursuing a big gorgeous goal pushes you to new heights and changes your life, because it shows you what is actually possible, and that encourages you to take another bold step toward the next pinnacle.

The 90 Percent: Where Luck and Hard Work Intersect

As an entrepreneur, you may be predisposed to attributing your success to luck, potentially diminishing your and your team's hard work. In fact, you exercise a special brand of resilience, risk taking, and dogged determination. You ride the highs and lows and, every day, make tough choices about what direction to head in. You constantly push yourself to learn more, to work in areas in which you feel underqualified and inexperienced— all in service of growing and nurturing a business.

So, what looks like luck is firmly anchored in the backbone of hard work—the blood, sweat, and tears of building. Just like an iceberg, luck sits on the top 10 percent you can see. What people don't see from the outside is the 90 percent, composed of hard work, building, decision making, and sleepless nights wondering if you've done the right thing.

Perhaps what luck really is, is taking hold of opportunity when it presents itself, accepting that bit of information, knowledge, support—whatever you need—and leveraging it into something bigger. What you make of opportunity rests in your own hands.

The Mechanics of a Big Gorgeous Goal

If the recipe for achieving that big gorgeous goal includes a dash of luck combined with several generous cups of hard work, what are the other ingredients? There are a few to consider.

A written record. Research reported by Mark Murphy shows that the more detailed you can be in your plans, the more likely you are to achieve them. As well, writing down the goal helps store it in your long-term memory. Once there, it is easier to remember, which increases the chances you will achieve and reach this goal. So, grab a notebook or open a file on your desktop and write down your big gorgeous goals. Be detailed. The more vivid the description, the better. Writing down the goal gives you a visual cue. Keep this written record in a safe place—you may want to refer to it when you need a reminder of the big picture.

Articulate what you need in place to reach your goal. Often, achieving a goal takes a village of effort. When I was starting my coaching business and I wanted to land corporate clients, I drew out what that looked like: How many clients did I need? How many corporations would I need as clients? How many people would I need to coach in each organization and over what time period? I tried to be as specific as possible, from outlining the contacts I would leverage to get in the door to crafting my pitch. I kept myself accountable by talking about the goal with my coach and my trusted friends and mentors.

Keeping a goal journal can be helpful. You can use the space to write about your feelings, resistance points, and progress. Ask yourself:

- Can I clearly define my big gorgeous goal?

- Am I feeling stuck? If so, why?

- What am I afraid of?

- Am I resisting anything? If so, what could be causing my resistance?

Over time, you will start to see how you hold yourself back. You may not be able to answer the questions above right away, and that's okay. What's important is the process of examining your goals. Set that big gorgeous goal and step toward it. Revisit your notes so that you can revise and hone the goal, and measure your progress against it.

Little steps. Once you've articulated your goal, break it down to inch along the path of doing it. Don't look up at the big goal too often lest you feel intimidated by how far you have to go. A big gorgeous goal can take months, or even years, to complete!

Tammy Barlette is a retired lieutenant colonel in the US Air Force and the founder of Athena's Voice, a speaking agency that highlights women veterans. She is a huge believer in the "little steps" method. Tammy relates it to looking up at a mountain and deciding that you want to go up it. You tuck your goal away and keep it safe, then take little steps on the trail as you ascend. "You can't look up at the mountain every five minutes or you will feel like you'll never get there," she said. "You can't keep staring at the big, wild goal. You will be like, *no way*. But you can say, 'I'm going to walk to that rock... I'm just going to walk for five minutes up.' Then you say, 'Okay, now I'm going to stop and see what's going on.'"

Tammy described the little steps she took the day she drove to the base for her pilot training. Nearing the base, she found herself right under the flight path of T-38s, the planes the US Air Force uses to train fighter pilots. Tammy said,

So, I'm like, "This is so cool! Look at their formation; they are flying so close to each other." Then I realize that their landing gear is down. I was like, "Wait, the wheels are down. What's going on here? Why are they still next to each other? Where's the..." and I see them land together. I was like, "What? No way. I can't do that." I hadn't even driven onto the base yet and I was deciding that I couldn't do it. Then I told myself: "Stop. Okay. Can I do that? I'm here. I'm qualified. And I'm just going to drive onto the base. I'm just going to find my room. I'm just going to go to class, get my gear—one step at a time. I got this. Little steps. This is what I'm going to do."

Bumps in the road. Don't let these throw you off! Deviations from the plan are normal. In fact, you should expect them. Goals that stretch over weeks, months, or years are bound to shift. Bumps are just more data points for you to gather and consider. They don't mean that your work is bad or worthless. When a goal seems to be going sideways, sit back and observe the situation. Move your focus from the tactical to the big picture and evaluate your plan. Would a slightly different path be better? Can you shift either the steps in the plan or the destination slightly to achieve something amazing?

Lori Weir is the CEO and cofounder of Four Eyes Financial. Her company was founded in late 2015 and has been growing quickly, with sales and the team doubling over the last year alone. Four Eyes has built a digital services platform for wealth management firms that need to be able to quickly show their work during regulatory audits. Lori has powerful views about how goals can shift and change. She said:

I don't have a looming view that success must look a certain way, or that if it doesn't look like that, I've failed. I have seen a lot of people thrown off by that mindset. I have no problem investing every aspect of myself in a goal and still being okay if it fails at the grandest level. I absolutely want it. I'm very competitive. I want to win. I want to succeed. But I don't base going forward on whether or not I'll achieve the exact outcome I originally planned. Sometimes I wish I had a standard operating procedure, but I tend to live my life in the innovation cycle.

Let it rest. Sometimes, you may even need to let a goal simmer on the back burner for some time as it develops. Alyssa Kerbel described letting a goal rest for more than two years, until it was ready to make its way into the world. Alyssa founded the Toronto-based children's fashion brand Mini Mioche more than a decade ago, with a mission to produce and sell locally made, ethically manufactured clothes in a way that aligned with her values. On a 2018 trip to New York City, near the end of a long line for tickets to the musical *Hamilton*, she and three others were approached by a random stranger, who gave them each a free ticket to the show, simply suggesting that they pay the kindness forward. She had an incredible time and afterward went to a bar with her notebook, where she developed an idea for a give-back program for her business. But at the time, she had to park it because there wasn't the bandwidth to take it on. She said:

> Then, during all the craziness of the pandemic, I felt so compelled to do something. I felt like I needed to get the website for the give-back program off the ground, that it was a resource the people needed then, in particular. They were at home, they were with their kids, and it was just the time for this information... So, I just needed to get it out there. I wasn't sure that anyone would even look at it, and you know, I didn't even really care. The site was far from perfect, but it was out there. I made sure that perfect wasn't the enemy of done, and I was confident that once it was out there in the world, I could tweak it as I went.
>
> And for all that time, I had no plan to make this happen... Everything just came together in an organic way,

without a very specific plan or timeline or steps. Sometimes you don't need that. Sometimes you do. And sometimes it's all about timing, and having the inspiration and the vision.

Big Influences

Many of the women I interviewed talked about how their upbringing influences how they think expansively about their goals. They have taken what they were given while growing up and used it as fuel for their big gorgeous goals.

BE Alink has always been drawn to concepts outside what most people think about, whether that's building schools in Afghanistan; working in Aceh, Indonesia, after the tsunami in 2004; or doing aid work in Africa. Incredibly down-to-earth and a questioner of systems, BE has created a movement around the company she founded, Alinker Inventions, which produces a revolutionary walking aid that places the user's experience at the center of mobility support. The ingenious device resembles a three-wheel bike, without pedals, that assists people with walking. A registered B Corp, Alinker uses crowdfunding to provide the device to those who can't afford it. Sponsors regularly fund the campaigns, and BE has attracted a celebrity following. BE's moral compass helps her determine where to put her energy. Then she builds community where she lands and focuses on developing new systems.

BE credits her father for presenting her with challenges to her thinking. Instead of telling her a bedtime story, her father would ask her to imagine that they lived in a three-story apartment, and then say, "If we turned it on its side by 90 degrees, what would we need to do to make it livable?" With the front window lying on the grass and the kitchen on the ceiling, they would step meticulously through all the alterations that would be needed to make the space habitable. BE sees this as her training for big-picture thinking. She had to lift up her view and consider the whole scenario, to think creatively and look for alternative ways to see what is "normal."

Diana Bishop broke many barriers as a journalist before becoming an entrepreneur. She was the first woman bureau chief for Asia for Canada's CTV News, and later became the Beijing bureau chief for NBC News before returning to Canada to cover Ottawa and international affairs. She later took a big leap out of journalism, focusing on helping people and corporations tell their stories through her business, The Success Story Program. She also tells her own story and talks about the influence of her family on her life. She spoke with me of the challenges of being a woman in a man's world and the pressures of living up to her family history. "My grandfather was World War I flying ace Billy Bishop," she told me. "I had this sense of 'I've got to be great somehow; how am I going to do that?' As a woman, I didn't have a voice growing up, and seeing my mother so contained in her role, it was important for me to find something where I had a voice. I think that's why I chose journalism, and especially broadcast journalism—because it gave me a voice."

Diana learned that the storytelling was most important to her, and it has been the thread that runs through all her endeavors. Through telling stories, she amplifies others' voices too, and unraveling their stories has helped her understand how to live up to her own name.

The founder of a resoundingly successful executive assistant recruitment agency, Priority VA, Trivinia Barber grew up with dreams of being the first person in her family to go to college. Her plans took a big turn when her grandmother was diagnosed with dementia and Alzheimer's disease, and Trivinia decided to stay home and care for her. Her college dreams faded and she took a different path, but still she yearned to create something more of herself. "It sort of dimmed the dream of being all the things, but I started to think, *How can I apply this to the work I'm doing now?*"

Your upbringing likely affects you too—your drive to succeed, your big dreams, the ways in which you view the world. Often, early experiences influence the "why"—the deeper purpose that drives us forward. The key is to understand that whatever you've experienced has value—your past is a resource. As you build your business, I encourage you to reflect on how your experiences can and do provide fuel for chasing your big gorgeous goals.

BIG GORGEOUS TAKEAWAYS

- Big gorgeous goals happen when a little luck combines with a lot of hard work.

- Writing about your goals will help you achieve them.

- You'll get to a big goal by taking little steps toward it.

- Expect that you'll need to revisit and recalibrate your goals.

4

THE INFLECTION POINT

How to Sense Into
and Navigate Change

in·flec·tion

/inˈflekSH(ə)n/ *noun*

a change of curvature from convex to concave at a particular point on a curve

AT MABEL'S LABELS, we always had an incredibly busy few weeks from early August to mid-September. It was back-to-school season, and that meant extremely high demand for labels as parents prepared their little ones for the adventures of a new school year.

We had built our own custom software for our production facility. And in the fateful year of 2011, as the company's leader of IT (with the sole qualification of being one of the company's founders—my background was in liberal arts and then finance!), I knew we were reaching the limits of its capacity. A small, persistent voice in the back of my head had been telling me for a while that we were going to need to change our systems. But not wanting to make major changes before the back-to-school rush, we tweaked a few things and counted on a wing and a prayer to get us through the season.

Needless to say, we were not prepared for the mad rush that was the mother of all back-to-school years—sales in 2011 went through the roof, with parents buying labels for their children in droves, and our production processes were outdated for the size of business we had become. During a rough few weeks, many of the team pulled all-nighters and worked extended hours to move the labels out the door and into the hands of our customers. As the head of IT, I saw our lack of capacity play out in front of my eyes, and it was incredibly stressful.

I knew that we had hit an inflection point: we couldn't meet our service standards for our customers and grow at the same time. We needed to make some major changes to upgrade the efficiency of the production facility. This kind of change was always nerve-racking, as we would have to enter into the unknown, and we worried about what else might break when we tried to fix the problem areas. But something in me knew, too, that if we made these changes, the future would be easier.

So, we did what we needed to do: we hired an expert in manufacturing efficiency, who helped us design a more accurate, more automated system that pushed out a higher volume and accommodated the growth of the business. It was a difficult few weeks, but we recovered and built something that helped us soar through our next busy season.

The 10 Percent: Moments of Pure Possibility

I often say that as soon as business starts feeling easy, an inflection point is coming.

On a graph in math, an inflection point is where the curvature of a line changes from concave to convex. In business, it's much the same—no matter how hard you work or how successful you are, inevitably you will reach a point when what got you there won't take you any further, and you need to change direction. This could mean learning new things, changing how you operate, taking on a bigger team, or just doing business differently.

Inflection points are like signals for you to lean in to your resilience and resourcefulness. The trouble is, if you're not careful, these points can sneak up on you. Maybe you notice a slow decline in sales, or you see a new trend emerging in your field and realize you have some catching up to do. Suddenly, what used to work isn't as effective as it once was. You may feel uncomfortable and uncertain about what to do next. Yet one of the risks is in doing nothing, giving in to the inertia that can develop when you're at a crossroads. So, becoming attuned to the rhythms of your business and when these points are imminent is important. The more you recognize and reflect on the changes in your business and in its milieu, the more you can strategize and get the help you need to shift directions.

If you resist inflection points, they can feel like a grind. But they are moments of pure possibility. Open up to different perspectives and ideas about what might work, what might happen if you take another path. Because there is no one "right" path to your goal. Sometimes, the best decision is to pivot and follow the opportunities.

Trivinia Barber became an experienced executive assistant in the field of online marketing. She was intuitive about what was needed as an EA, and saw many possibilities for the EA to form a team with the executive they reported to, leveraging their joint efforts into something that was greater than the sum of its parts. Realizing there was a market for this, she founded Priority VA to bring her methods to many. Trivinia told me that she sometimes feels she goes from one inflection point to another. She said,

It has been a journey, and it has not been easy. I used to wish that someone had told me how hard this is. It isn't just having a good idea and then all the magical things happen. A lot of mental capacity must go into running a business. I used to think that if we were good to people and did what we said, everything was going to work. Now I know that it's trial by fire, and that leading constantly means growing as a human. I didn't realize that for a long time.

The 90 Percent: Planning Will Ease You through the Curve

Some simple principles will help you navigate change, build resilience, and foster a learning mindset to ease you through inflection points.

Take Stock

Often, at an inflection point, tension is in the air. Something doesn't feel quite right, and putting your finger on what's happening can be hard. The challenge is that to navigate an inflection point well, you've got to clearly define the problem so that you can effectively solve it.

It may feel counterintuitive, but usually the first step is to sit back and contemplate. Often, approaching an inflection point, you will hear that small voice in your head, the one that keeps you up at night, that notices things are either changing or about to.

This voice is one of wisdom, so don't ignore it! Tune in to it in whatever way works best for you—walk in nature, take a few days off, or go to a yoga class. Often, stepping away from screens and making space to think works best. Getting lost in a puzzle (crossword, sudoku, or jigsaw) can help too. Allowing your mind to wander opens up creativity so you can think more expansively.

Without judgment, examine whatever random thoughts pop up. Jot them down in a notebook if you need to. Ask yourself questions too. Are you feeling stuck? Like something isn't working? Or is it that things are moving so fast that you need to take a breath and evaluate? Write down your answers. Look for themes and patterns in your thinking to determine what has you feeling a little off.

Once you have a clear idea about the issue at hand, you can move on to planning how to respond. Don't skip this step. If you don't define the problem clearly, you'll waste time in the next steps and likely end up having to take stock again.

Plan

Inflection points often start off feeling like a grind, and then, once you tip over the edge into action, you feel as if you're running a race. So, before you get to that point, pause and formulate a plan. Advance warning: you will feel like you don't have time for this, but it is *exactly* the time to pause, whether for a few minutes or a few hours. A plan will help you define a rhythm to where you are going and prioritize the next steps with clarity so you'll move forward faster.

Planning doesn't have to be difficult. You can use an easy tool to funnel your thinking:

1 **Write down the three most important factors about your problem.**

- Prioritize these factors.

- For each factor, note the first three steps to address the factor.

2 **Set completion dates for each step.**

3 **Evaluate the plan, noting as many details as you can.**

- Are there critical items that may block your progress?

- Does anyone need to be informed or brought into the circle of knowledge to help you progress on this?

- Are there any potential collisions with other colleagues, teams, or departments?

- What can you delegate to your team? How will you track that?

- Who do you need to bring in to help you execute? Who in your network can be a resource to teach you? Do you need to hire someone?

Now you have a road map of priorities: a living, breathing document you can update as often as you need to. Nothing stays the same for long. Making sure that your plan continues to serve you is an important part of the process.

Planning at inflection points is also about being creative and working with what you have, finding new ways to operate. Vicki Saunders, CEO and founder of SheEO, concurs. This groundbreaking, radically generous organization began in Canada with the idea that five hundred women would contribute one thousand dollars each to a fund that would loan women and non-binary founders capital to grow their businesses.

Vicki describes herself as a doer. "I'm not a stay-up-in-the-clouds kind of person. I function at both ends," she told me. Vicki has a stellar ability to hold a big vision while doing the groundwork. This isn't easy, but it is an extremely valuable skill set.

Although she's had detractors, Vicki's vision for SheEO remains big and transformative for the global economy. Of pursuing her goals, she said: "It has been whole bunch of baby steps along the way. I have done a ton of experimentation. Trying things out. Iterate, tweak. I could literally write a book about how my whole life has been a failure. I've literally failed at everything." Outsiders may marvel at everything she has done, but she often felt as though her ambitions outstripped her accomplishments. Now, she believes she is closer than ever to the version of success she sees in her mind. The global growth of the SheEO network, in five countries, with passionate and dedicated women who are using their capital to fund women entrepreneurs with start-ups, has created a movement. It is gaining breadth and speed with each cohort of female-founded companies that SheEO supports.

Hold the Big Picture Daily

Taking stock and planning are not one-and-done endeavors. Regularly thinking big about any problem you're tackling keeps you nimble and builds resilience. Some tips to help you do this are:

- Schedule time at the end of each day to focus on the big picture. (Some days, you may need to do this every hour!)

- Review your plans and the next steps.

- Keep aligning your plan with the big picture; adjust and refine it for tomorrow.

- Continue to look for the next steps, and build out the plan beyond those initial steps, so that you get to completion.

- Communicate with those who are dependent on the plan— you don't want to reach a big milestone and find you've left the team a few steps back.

You can also use this time to work through problems that are harder to define. When your gut is telling you that something isn't going the way it should be, but you can't quite put your finger on what, make all the notes you can, raise your antennae to what might be happening, and then step away. Allow some space to think on the problem. Exercise. Sleep on it. Talk to people you trust—your peers, team, advisors—and listen to them. Return to it the next day. As your notes accumulate, look for themes. What consistently comes up? Does that tell you anything?

This process can take as little as fifteen minutes a day. Don't skip it! If you create the right habits and practice them regularly, it will get easier to see the problems. You may notice a long-entrenched issue or one with roots somewhere completely unexpected. Stick with the process of expanding your thinking. Slowly, a picture will start to emerge.

Dreaming Big

Some inflection points are grueling reminders of how difficult it is to overcome certain hurdles. But each offers learning that can be applied to the next. To deal with them, you can build strategies based on your unique strengths. Maintaining a learning mindset, creating a plan, and holding the big picture in mind are common habits of high-achieving women.

You can prepare for such moments by regularly moving outside your comfort zone to get comfortable with being uncomfortable. This builds the muscle of resilience that allows you to pause, reflect, and examine the circumstances. Deliberately stepping into discomfort requires a kind of "stick-with-it-ness" that values putting in the hard work and finding the tools to keep going.

Sandra (Sandy) Stosz, leadership coach and author of *Breaking Ice & Breaking Glass*, joined the Coast Guard about two years after the Coast Guard Academy had opened to women. She started out at the bottom, as a cadet, in a four-year college program, and eventually became the first female graduate of the Coast Guard Academy to achieve the rank of vice admiral in the US Coast Guard. Sandy told me, "When you start at the bottom, you know what it's like to have to dig and scrape. I literally cleaned toilets. We had scullery duty, where we did the dishes. Sometimes, the ship would be keeled all the way over on its side and there we were, trying to do the dishes."

After Sandy graduated the academy, she was commissioned as an officer—at the lowest rank—and was assigned to an icebreaker berthed at Long Beach, California. On this ship, she sailed to the Antarctic. She told me:

It was spectacular, the opportunity of a lifetime, to see some of the Pacific Islands on the way, stop in New Zealand, and then spend several months in Antarctica, breaking ice for science missions and supporting the navy base that's down there. This motivated me to continue with the Coast Guard. The combination of hard work and motivation are important... You do all that hard work; then you get to the next level and you get to do something exhilarating, like deploying to Antarctica. That motivated me to continue to move up. When I graduated from the academy, I never wanted to be an admiral. I just wanted to pursue opportunities in the Coast Guard, to stretch myself beyond my comfort zone.

When you're at sea, Sandy explained, you are tired and wet, cold and hungry—and scared. But when you are amenable to discomfort, you grow. "Every time you take on something more challenging that you have to reach for," she said, "you're standing on a solid foundation. Sure, you're going to fail here and there, but your foundation will not erode from under you."

BIG GORGEOUS TAKEAWAYS

- Usually, when the business starts to feel "easy," a big change is on the horizon.

- Problems often have more than one solution, and you've got to work to define the problem.

- Focus on the big picture every day.

- Become comfortable with being uncomfortable to build resilience.

5

FOUNDER AS LEADER

How to Be the Boss of a Stellar Workplace

lead·er

/ˈlēdər/   *noun*

the person who leads or commands a group,
organization, or country

N O ONE TAUGHT me how to manage people. Before starting Mabel's Labels, I had never led a team. And when we started the company, it was just us four cofounders, although eventually we hired a team.

From early on, my cofounders and I kept different schedules. These were based on our roles, our other obligations (some of us had full-time jobs when we started the business), and our current priorities. When we hired staff, we needed independent workers with good problem-solving skills who could make decisions and keep moving. In other words, we gave our team the freedom to get shit done. The by-product of this was that we developed a culture of accountability. People weren't afraid to make decisions and to back them up with their reasoning. Yes, sometimes things went wrong, but it was always a learning experience that built even better skills for decisions in the future.

When the company was small, we had a real family atmosphere, and everyone who worked for us was as invested as we were in growing our business. Those were such fun days with those early team members. As the business grew, the time came when I had to manage some of our people. And I quickly realized that I didn't know how to give feedback very well (in fact, I probably avoided it), and when it came to formally setting expectations and holding my team accountable, I had lots of learning to do.

I also struggled to delegate effectively. I would dole out tasks and projects with little direction. On the day a project was due, I would be full of expectation. But most of the time, I didn't like what came back to me. For a while, I thought it was easier to do it myself, until I realized that I was working way too much, and that my attitude wasn't going to create a sustainable business (or a happy team). I had to learn how to delegate well, and to practice it!

The 10 Percent:
Learn to Be the Leader of a Culture That Works for You

As the founder, you need to make sure your leadership sets the tone you want for your business. Culture, after all, flows from the top down. Although some people have a natural skill set that lends itself to leadership, if you have no training or previous experience with it, you're likely going to need to develop the skills to lead great teams.

You may have started your company because you had a great idea that led you to create a business that would solve a problem you saw in the world. One of the ironies of success is that when your company grows, you end up with "big company problems" that can include HR issues, team motivation and engagement, and a lack of delegation or leverage to get more done through the people who work for you.

Creating a culture of accountability in which the team makes great decisions and is engaged in the outcomes is the dream of every business owner. To do this, you've got to determine your own role and priorities. As the owner or founder and leader, you've got to set the pace, give effective feedback, communicate your vision, and delegate work well to develop a successful culture.

The 90 Percent: Motivate, Set the Pace, Delegate

With practice and intention, you can develop excellent leadership skills. Adopting some key techniques will ensure that the work flows down to the right levels of the team and will give you the freedom to steer the strategy and leverage the team to success.

The Motivator-in-Chief

The leader of any organization must initiate and lay out a vision for the team to follow. Although teams usually want autonomy to make decisions, they also want a *boss* who leads them forward. They want someone who communicates about progress toward the goals—where they are going and how they are going to get there. They need someone who cheers them on and celebrates the successes with them. And yes, they also want someone who cries with them when things don't go as hoped or planned, and who rallies them to take on the world again.

Part of your job as leader is to communicate in ways that land and ensure that everyone is working toward the same ultimate goal. This means articulating messages clearly—and usually more often than you expect to. You also need to appeal to different people in differing ways. Are some of your team members visual? Setting up a whiteboard to track progress or using images to describe the work might be what they need.

Others may understand emails and spreadsheets better. Still others may need to hear you speak about the work and goals. Figure out what your team needs or hire someone to help you communicate so that the messages get across.

Giving constructive feedback is another important part of the boss' role as motivator-in-chief. A common mistake is not addressing issues as they arise. Waiting until the next meeting or staff review to give feedback makes it more difficult to deliver—and for others to receive. When you deliver a performance review, there should be no surprises. Everything the team member hears should already have been discussed.

Giving constructive feedback can be uncomfortable, but it becomes easier with practice—and it is your obligation because it helps the team produce better work and sets the tone for a culture of continuous improvement.

There are many techniques for giving feedback. When in doubt, try these simple methods.

Two positives and a negative. Give two (or three) positive comments for every negative or constructive piece of feedback. Let's say you hired an incredibly talented graphic designer, but he often does not deliver on time. In conversation, you might say: "I love the work you produced for the back-to-school campaign. The graphic design was on the mark, and the drawings were aligned with our brand. I noticed, though, that you delivered the work late. This affected the rest of the team, because they needed to reprioritize their work to meet the deadline. What can I do to support you meeting the deadline next time?"

Focus on performance. Focus on the team member's performance, not on their personality. Give fact-based, on-point feedback. Preparing your remarks beforehand is also useful to ensure that you are clear about what want to give feedback on. Be prepared to nonjudgmentally explain your point of view and to listen to theirs. When you do this, give feedback based on performance, and stick to the facts. Don't dip into your opinion. Consider the difference between statements like, "I think you're lazy and incommunicative" and "You sent your report two days later than the date we agreed on and you didn't let me know it would be late." Using fact-based language is key.

The objective is to motivate your team members to improve, for the benefit of the business. You may need to consciously learn the skill of giving feedback, and getting it right the first time is rare. But with practice, you can learn to do it effectively much of the time. Your teams will improve and team members will even learn how to give one another feedback. Seek out role models and watch them closely as you cultivate this skill set. You likely know people who are great with their teams, so don't be shy to ask them how they give feedback and what is important to them in that process.

The Pacesetter

With a strategic plan in motion, your job is to set the pace and keep your team on track. What does the business need to accomplish each week, month, and quarter? You or another team member may manage the mechanics, which could include breaking down the goals into manageable bites, designating appropriate checkpoints and milestones, and communicating clearly about progress and next steps.

Here, again, is where a whiteboard can be useful, to provide a visual reference for major project milestones everyone can see. The whiteboard can be a place to check off completed items and to refer to the team's progress against goals. It allows for open conversations about how the work is going. The whiteboard can be an actual physical object—in your office, say—but there are plenty of effective virtual options as well. Choose the format based on how your team best learns and responds.

As the pacesetter, you must recognize when to adjust plans, which you might have to do because of shifting priorities, projects that balloon beyond the budget, or about a million other reasons. No project unfolds exactly as planned. As things shift and change, your job is to know the limits of the team. No one wants to lead a team into the land of disengagement and burnout.

Communication is key to a pacesetter's success. Daily check-ins are sometimes useful, for any project. Weekly emails and monthly reports or meetings such as town halls keep people on track, as do quick rewards for team members who go beyond the necessary. There are so many ideas for this! The key is to bring problems to the surface quickly. Discussion about how to solve them rallies the group.

The Delegator-in-Chief

Delegation is paramount to success. Leveraging the collective power of your team allows you to keep your eyes on the long-term vision instead of sinking into the weeds. Delegating well—ensuring that your team knows what to do, what success looks like, and the delivery expectations—will increase your capacity for higher-level tasks. Your team's engagement level will also rise accordingly; they will be better functioning and more engaged—ready to conquer the world with you.

You may intellectually grasp that delegating frees your time and brain space, but in practice, it isn't easy! At Mabel's, as I grew my teams, I realized that I was struggling to give up control. On reflection, I saw that this was, in part, tied to my expectations. I assumed my team members would produce the work exactly as I envisioned it. But mostly, they didn't. As I mentioned, at first I adopted the attitude that doing the work myself was more efficient, and I stopped delegating. This resulted in my being overworked and my team being disengaged. It wasn't a scalable option. And so, over time, I learned the six key steps to effective delegation:

1 Before delegating, pause. Consider the desired outcome for the task. Thoroughly describe what success looks like.

2 Outline the task. Make sure all parties involved understand the deliverables. Clearly articulate what is included in the task and what is not, so that the project doesn't balloon.

3 Communicate a delivery date. Consider the scope of the project and consult with the people executing the task to set realistic timelines.

4 Designate checkpoints. Use key milestones as ways to evaluate progress, share information, and course-correct. The number of checkpoints should be relative to the size of the project.

5 Define the important alignment criteria. The major stakeholders must agree on the most important criteria for the project. Identify those spots where if you aren't in agreement the project will be at risk, and evaluate whether the project is achieving alignment at the checkpoints.

6 Give feedback. Give feedback at the end of the project. This ensures that you remain timely and prompt with any praise or opportunities for improvement.

This process isn't complicated, but it does help capture, in writing, each step at the start of the project, so you're clear and thorough in communication. This improves outcomes.

Imagine what could happen without such a process. You've likely been through a few such scenarios. Let's say you ask a team member to build of a small piece of software, such as adding a small button to your CRM (Client Relationship Management) software. You sketch out a high-level target and give the developer a week to complete the project. Off they go, coding the requested feature and adding the button. At the end of the week, they proudly deliver the feature. As you review their work, you realize that, because there was no interim feedback during the development process, the feature button is placed awkwardly, and it's difficult to find. The developer considers the project complete and needs to move on to other things. But you need the project corrected. At least part of their workweek has been wasted, and unless you can free up more time for the developer, you'll be stuck with an oddly placed button. Not an ideal outcome, and a reason why figuring out the alignment criteria in any project is important.

Delegating using the steps outlined above, you can better avoid problems:

1 **Before delegating, pause.** Consider the desired outcome for the task.
   * This feature button needs to be easy to locate, click through to the proper page, and automate the collection of customer email addresses.

2 **Outline the task.**
   * Place the button prominently on the site.

- Write code that enables an auto-fill function. Once the user enters their email address and clicks the button, the email address should populate the customer screen, the shipping notification box, and the carrier tracker integration.

3 Communicate a delivery date.
- The button is due in one week.

4 Designate checkpoints.
- Send it for review and approval when the wireframe is complete.
- Send a complete draft of the approved design.

5 Define the important alignment criteria.
- Team alignment on the logistics—where the button will be on the screen, what it does, and where it links to (what opens when you click on it).
- Management alignment on all of the above plus approval of the work effort involved.

6 Give feedback.
- I appreciate how creatively you integrated my initial feedback, and that you hit the deadline.

Can you see how this process would circumvent misunderstandings and wasted efforts? Establishing and articulating what you want is worth the time it takes. No one is going to complete the task exactly as you would. But follow these steps and it will be done. And not by you!

Delegating is a key component to scaling yourself up. For one, it frees up your time for big thinking and dreaming. Plus, your team grows as you grow.

Leading with a Big Heart

Learning skillful leadership is a journey that you'll likely travel through all your years of entrepreneurship. Building a high-performing team requires openness, hiring the right people who contribute positively to the culture, bringing in different viewpoints, and leveraging the skills of your talent to reach your big gorgeous goals.

Shaina Azad is the founder and CEO of SUVA Beauty, a cutting-edge cosmetics company known for its bright, bold colors and its neon graphic liner that disrupted the industry. As a makeup artist in Vancouver, British Columbia, Shaina saw an opportunity to develop the products she felt were missing from the market. One item turned into two, then two to four. Now, her business has a full product line with global distribution channels. Shaina spoke to me about the kind of decisions she makes as the leader, and where and how teams are integral to her work. "For our branding and brand identity, the goals are more like tunnel vision," she said. "I need to be clear about what is right for us as a brand and a company, and not listen to many different opinions. But for the business side—product planning, forecasting, marketing, sales—well then, I drop that tunnel vision because I need to be completely aware of everything happening, of all the moving pieces. This is where it's important to have a really strong team."

Shaina described the process of learning how to delegate and how delegation is an ongoing practice that supports big thinking.

When you start out, unless you have tons of money to back you, you are wearing all the hats in the company.

You can't maintain that view, or else you aren't really going to grow. So I've always had this mindset of being able to give things to someone else. I need to manage my team properly and effectively, but I can't manage all the smaller pieces if I'm going to chase the big vision and goals for my company. I'm constantly thinking about how I can break pieces off my own position and create roles for my team to take them on. I need to get away from being caught up in the day-to-day and keep that big vision in mind. I have the fire in me to be able to reach as many markets as possible with my brand. To do that, I need to keep myself at a strategic level in the business.

BIG GORGEOUS TAKEAWAYS

- Founders, owners, or entrepreneurs can lead a culture that supports their vision for the business.

- Culture flows from the top down. Skillful leadership will create a culture of accountability by motivating teams, setting the pace of work and growth, and delegating well.

- Delegating the right work to the right people frees your time for strategic and big thinking so that you can steer the organization.

6

WISE COUNSEL

How to Invest in Yourself

in·vest

/in'vest/ *verb*

to make use of for future benefits or advantages

ABOUT SEVEN YEARS into my journey of building Mabel's Labels, I reached a point when everything felt hard. I had begun managing our IT and finance teams, and my cofounders and I were facing challenges as a growing business. We felt a lot of responsibility for our employees' paychecks. We needed to make sure that the sales kept coming in, and that we would have the cash to grow and thrive.

Because I didn't have a formal background in tech, I often felt that I was helplessly grasping at the right choices. I knew this couldn't possibly be the best way forward. Until then, I had spent most of my time focusing internally, working on building the business and running many important day-to-day functions. As the business grew and became more complex, the teams in the offices of Mabel's Labels became unable to answer all the questions that arose. I concluded that I was going to need to expand my network to secure the advice of those who had already traveled this path. I also realized that over time, the need for advice would shift and change depending on the size of the business, the current problem to solve, and how we imagined things unfolding as we progressed toward our goals.

As a team, my cofounders and I had always been good at working with advisors. We found people who were smarter than us and solicited their help as mentors or to act as paid advisors. However, stepping out alone to seek outside help with my personal professional journey was new to me. It felt edgy at first, but I was pleasantly surprised by all the options. Sponsors, mentors, and my own privy council would all become a part of my "outside" support team as I invested in myself.

First, a friend from my university days who worked at an innovation center connected me with people in the field, and I familiarized myself with what they had to offer. I attended innovation center events, met people working in the tech space, and built a network.

Soon, I met a couple of people who had founded tech companies and actually *did* have technical backgrounds. They became sounding boards for me and vetted information, parsing the good from the bad. Their input helped me understand the available options for tech decisions, why my team was recommending a certain path, and the pros and cons of it. Because I had a safe space and the benefit of their perspectives, I made better and more efficient decisions. I could return to my internal team as a leader and feel like I had some background as we navigated important business decisions. I also gained confidence to ask questions and dig for information from the team as we planned.

When another innovation center opened much closer to where I lived, I started attending events there and met many others working in the same area as I did, and again, they were often more experienced than I was. I eventually joined the organization's board, furthering my connections and contributing to the local start-up community. This role lasted for more than eight years and solidified my network to leverage as I moved on to new and different things.

The 10 Percent: Invest in You

When you inevitably enter into unknown territory, it often happens unexpectedly, and realizing you are stuck may take some time. You need to discover new ways to invest in yourself, to build your capacity to grow. The right combination of mentors, coaches, and advisors will support your development. Establishing this takes effort and networking, but the time spent doing so will be invaluable.

Unfortunately, in business and life, you really can't google all the answers! Building relationships with fellow entrepreneurs is another key to success. People who are going through the same things as you are know what the road looks like and often have words of advice and encouragement.

The 90 Percent:
Build the Priceless Resource of a Wide, Diverse Network

Creating support systems will build your confidence to go after your big gorgeous goal. Finding mentors, coaches, and a special group of women advisors (what I call a privy council) is an important step in investing in yourself and your business.

The Mentor

Mentors are those who give you advice and counsel. The network I've built has helped me many times over as I've wrestled with problems or questions. But finding these valuable people isn't always easy. You've got to keep in mind how to open yourself to those who will lift you up. To begin, you can:

- Look for organizations and associations that support women founders.

- Join a local networking group.

- Go to events and build your network.

- Give freely when others ask for help.

When you find someone who has expertise you would like to learn more about, invite them for coffee or lunch. Take the opportunity to assess their fit for you as a prospective mentor. You may just need that one lunch or coffee to ask the relevant questions related to their knowledge and skills. However, if you find you want to create a longer-term mentorship with them, you need to ask for it. Often, mentors will work with you in return for lunch or dinner a handful of times a year.

Women in business should always be looking for ways to help other women. Keep that awareness alive as you seek out others who believe the same, as they will help you carve a brilliant path. Sandy Stosz, the retired vice admiral of the US Coast Guard whom you met in chapter 4, described being strategic about seeking out mentors, and an unexpected benefit of mentorship. "You need to reach out to people who you see as allies," she said. "And not just to support you to get to the top but also to support your work for the whole team so that everybody wins, and the organization wins. Everybody working with you achieves their full potential. Oh, and by the way, you rise also. Reaching out your hand, to ask for help or to bring somebody else up to where you are, benefits you."

Karen Grant is the chief operating officer of Equation Angels and has founded several angel investing groups. She noted the cyclical nature of relationships throughout her career. In one such instance, she sat on the board of an innovation organization and met a person who became a true believer in her talent and skills and mentored her along the way.

A few years after they sat on the board together, this person invested in Karen's latest start-up. Even after the start-up failed, he hired Karen to write a proposal for a government grant that would build an organization to cultivate entrepreneurs and start-up companies. When the organization successfully received funding, Karen was recruited to start Angel One Network so that those start-ups had somewhere to go for funding as they grew and expanded. Their relationship, which began with mentoring, lasted many years.

Karen spoke to me about how integrity plays a vital role in fostering beneficial mentor relationships. She said, "I've been blessed by a phenomenal number of fans who appreciate my candor and trust my willingness and integrity to do what I say I'll do. I think you benefit from the reputation you have left behind you, so I have been careful with my integrity." In fact, Karen credits her integrity for the reappearance of people in her life multiple times, presenting different opportunities.

Karen's experience suggests the value of seeking out various mentors and advisors over the seasons of a career. Some will get you to a certain point, then pass the baton to others for the next leg of the journey. Others will remain for a longer time. All are equally valuable.

The Coach

Once I had firmly established mentors in my circle and was regularly networking and attending events, I needed more dedicated work on my leadership skills. Mabel's had reached an inflection point—what had grown the business so far wasn't going to drive it to where we wanted it to go. To lead the business to a new level, I needed to be able to guide team members to do the groundwork to fulfill my vision so that I could spend more time on strategy. This is a significant shift, moving from a "doing" role to one of thinking, directing, and holding people accountable. I needed guidance and support for this transition.

I began playing with the idea of hiring a coach, talking to people I trusted about it. An advisor who was working with my cofounders and me at the time recommended someone. About a week later at a conference for women entrepreneurs, one of my business partners and I gathered a small group together for dinner. That evening, I was seated next to someone I had just met. Our conversation turned to coaching, and I mentioned that I was looking for a coach. She immediately and enthusiastically recommended hers—the same person our advisor had suggested!

At an event the next day, I was seated at a table with eight other women entrepreneurs. As we chatted, one woman mentioned having a coach, whom she spoke about in glowing terms. I asked for the person's name—and, once again, the referral was for that same coach.

Since this was the third time this coach had been recommended to me, I felt that the stars were aligning and that I had better book a meeting with her. I did, and it resulted in a long-term working relationship. I've been with her since 2011 and still have sessions today.

My coach became a sounding board for me and my ideas. We work through different options and she contributes a view that shows me a bigger picture or an angle I haven't yet considered. Coaching sessions are a safe space where I work out my thinking. During my time at Mabel's, this meant I was better prepared to present a comprehensive, cohesive picture when I met with my team or cofounders about something important.

Her experience as both a coach and a senior executive guided me to lift my thinking to a new level, to get out of the weeds, and to shed my internal culture of doing. I began to build deeper trust with my team members and grow them, too, so that they could execute on the many priorities of the business. I learned better hiring skills—how to select people who truly allowed me to step away from doing so that I could work on strategy.

The coaching relationship looks at all areas of life: business, family, home, and the whole person. Working with a coach can teach you many things about yourself. It can broaden your perspective and, with a good coach, over time, teach you to be a coach for yourself, too, integrating the skill of analysis—turning problems around and examining them from all angles.

The Privy Council

At that dinner I mentioned above, I discovered that many of the women around the table were facing the same issues I was in building a business while raising a family. We thought like entrepreneurs, and we were also busy driving kids to soccer practice and dance classes, going to parent-teacher interviews, nurturing our children, and managing the details of caring for a home. Most of the men I met through my IT networking were not dealing with the same pressures.

I realized that to thrive, I needed to keep developing my resources beyond the four walls of the Mabel's Labels office, building a network of big thinkers who pushed me to be bold in my thinking about the business.

And so, over several years I developed a group that I call my privy council. I looked for women who I could trust and relate to, who would listen to my ideas and offer sound advice about them. I sought out women who could understand what I was facing because they were facing similar issues. At networking events and social occasions, I noticed others who craved connection and a network of support and camaraderie. We started with dinners and began somewhat organically, but over time we became a tightly knit group that gathers, troubleshoots, and dreams together.

We lean on each other in good times and bad. We have gone on retreats together where we focus on idea development, sometimes even "gamifying" it. For example, we might come up with one hundred ideas for a business, think one might be "it," and run with it for a few weeks. If we realize that none of us is going to get the idea off the ground (so many other priorities!), we reset and start over again. This big thinking together helps me see the world in different ways. It's also fun, and the laughs, support, and understanding combined with questioning to improve and innovate fills my cup.

I highly recommend you seek out the support of other women entrepreneurs who are outside the box you create for yourself. Develop a resource that doesn't believe in the confining walls, ceilings, or any other self-imposed limitations but does believe in you and the gifts you have for the world. Creating your own privy council will require an investment of time and energy to get it off the ground and keep it alive. But consider the value of support from a group of women entrepreneurs who see you in all your messy glory and potential and get what you're going through, who believe in you and what you are capable of.

Friendships need feeding and care, too, and you'll want to give as much as you receive to your privy council. So, you may need to say no to other things to create space for it. Really, it's all about priorities for yourself and your own growth and development.

Investing Big in You

Founder of SheEO Vicki Saunders, whom you met in chapter 4, said, "You can make things hard, or you can follow the energy. Following the energy leads to finding your people. Once you find them, they bring in their people and things grow." When Vicki finds someone with whom she has that soul connection in the first five minutes, she asks them, "Who are five other people like you who I don't already know?"

This tool has helped Vicki grow her network of people who are *like-spirited*. The beauty of this is that they aren't *like-minded*. They all think differently, and that has been key to developing her vision. Building a network of people who can challenge you may push you outside your comfort zone—but remember, that's a good thing!

Janet Kestin and Nancy Vonk climbed the corporate ladder, creating for themselves support systems that consisted of mentors and others on whom they could rely along the way. Eventually, they became co-chief creative officers at marketing and branding firm Ogilvy & Mather in Toronto. They were also named among *Ad Age*'s 100 Most Influential Women in

Advertising in 2012. When they decided to leave their corporate careers to found Swim, an entrepreneurial endeavor that gives leaders tools to lead with creativity and humanity, Ogilvy became their first client. Starting a business is daunting enough, and Nancy and Janet were writing a book at the same time: a huge investment of time and brain space.

Fortunately for them, they had an amazing editor, who would drop off little notes and gifts on their front porches, always keeping in touch and letting them know that the book was important and they were valued. Janet told me it was

> like having a beautiful ghost in our machine. We had our will and desire to achieve our goals, but we were incredibly fortunate that we always had people who were there for us all the way along. They were different types of people, in completely different roles, with completely different relationships to us, but they wanted us to succeed. I think there are the mythical success-against-all-odds types, but the majority of people who do impressive things get there with the help of others. And that often goes missing in the storytelling of what's happened.

Nancy added, "You know, when you have those moments of seeing yourself as low in capability and potential, you can make your biggest strides when someone just gets in your face and says, 'You are more than you think.'"

On your path to achieving big gorgeous goals, seeking help and others' expertise broadens your knowledge and builds your confidence. However, you've also got to know when to stop gathering opinions and advice for your own future. You must discern when you're asking for more input because you haven't heard what you want to yet. There is a fine balance between listening to others and mistrusting your instincts. Invest in yourself through mentorship, coaching, and the like, with the objective of becoming more self-assured and capable, rather than becoming overly reliant on what other people think.

Journalist and author Diana Bishop's formula for investing in herself involves research, seeking advice, and self-reflection. When she needs to level up, she keeps her eye on a long-term plan while gathering information and expertise. First, she investigates the topic of concern (this is where her journalism training comes in handy) and takes extensive notes about what she learns. She then hires a subject-matter expert to advise her. At each forward step, she evaluates her next move. To ensure she's holding a high-level view of her career, she hosts a retreat with herself every quarter, spending time in a location away from her office (even a coffee shop works) and evaluating her progress toward her big goals and plans. Building in this time for self-reflection and calibration of her plans allows her to keep the perspective at a higher level.

A change of scenery and a technology diet allows her to do some blue-sky thinking. "It's amazing, you know, how simple it becomes when you get away from the house or your computer to do that," she said. "I try not to get freaked out by the big idea. I try to organize it in a logical way, and do one thing at a time, and it becomes so much more fun."

BIG GORGEOUS TAKEAWAYS

- Networks are made up of different facets. Mentors, coaches, and a privy council can help you to grow as a leader.

- Take the plunge and find those trusted people who lift you up.

- Building a network takes time, but it's worth the effort.

7

THE NUMBERS GAME

What You Need
to Know to Profit

prof·it

/ˈpräfət/

a financial gain, especially the difference between the amount earned and the amount spent in buying, operating, or producing something

O F THE HUNDREDS of founders I have met and worked with over the years, inevitably the reason they decided to start a business was to solve a problem in the world.

This was certainly the case for us at Mabel's Labels. We created our business to solve the problem of the lost and found. We helped parents stay organized and made it so their kids' things returned home again at the end of a long day. Caregivers, camp counselors, and teachers (and many others) loved how the labels worked because the lost and found was emptier and the items that did end up there were easily returned to their proper owners.

Quickly, we realized that many of the organizations that valued our products were also in need of funds. So, we initiated a fundraising program and assigned unique URLs to the organizations, which affiliated families could use to order labels. In return, the organizations received 20 percent of those sales in commissions. We promoted the program by attending trade shows for camp staff and owners, educators, and early-childhood professionals. This program allowed us to crack new markets, grow our name, and explain our business.

Why did we need to explain? Well, in being first to market, people didn't know labeling existed the way we were doing it. Iron-on or sew-in clothing labels had been around forever, but the idea of labels that were durable and sticky was novel. New moms, in particular, were on a learning curve and we continuously needed to conquer it. The beauty of this market is that babies are being born every day (even every minute, every second) and so it's constantly refreshing. This was a benefit, but also meant that our marketing team was making an ongoing effort to educate our target market about labeling and why they should buy our products.

As we grew various programs, ensuring that new initiatives were profitable to the company became increasingly important. At first, profitability was relatively easy to assess. We had few staff, and we were running a fairly simple business. But it was never easy for us to pinpoint exact costs, because we produced our labels in volume. So, we used high-level costing, and it worked for a long time. But when the business became more complex, we needed to dig deeper and figure out costing on a more granular level.

Assessing profitability can be a challenge for many businesses. At Mabel's, we ran into trouble figuring out what software would best provide the metrics we wanted and needed to run the business well. The quest to accurately price our products turned out to be quite a long journey.

The 10 Percent: Know What You Don't Know

Pricing makes you or breaks you. In the early days of your business, you may use some napkin math and get away with it. Napkin math is, as it sounds, working out some basic numbers in a rough sort of way. These are often high level and give you a picture of the ballpark you're playing in. But napkin math will only get you so far. Sooner or later, you will need to be able to dive deep and understand why your numbers do or don't add up.

Correctly setting your prices and understanding how they affect your overall bottom line is crucial to your success. Taking an unprofitable deal is *not* a sustainable business model, and neither is taking the deal and thinking that you'll raise prices or drive costs down later—no matter how tempting it seems in the moment. So, you've got to know your numbers, as well as know when you need help to get them right.

The 90 Percent: Build a Team You Can Learn From

Foundational to any business is a solid system for finances, including bookkeeping and accounting. This is one area where you don't want to mess around. I highly encourage you to hire skilled people to establish and execute these for you, if you don't have the skills yourself. To assess your profitability and pricing, you need to be able to accurately see the inflow and outflow of cash.

Thankfully, at Mabel's, we had the foresight to hire great finance people, both inside and outside the company, who helped us get started. As a former financial planner, I had a numbers background, but I had never looked at official financial statements for my own business, and the entries in our books looked backward to me because debits and credits are reversed in accounting and banking. It was also pretty clear that my numbers background would not be sufficient for the long haul of building the business. So, my cofounders and I set about building an internal and external finance team that could support the business—growing the top line and managing costs and expenses, looking for better deals, and spending our money wisely. These were all central to our success.

Our accountant set up a spreadsheet for us to regularly enter in the numbers to keep up to date. This gave us the foundation we needed to make educated decisions as we ran our business. It gave the employees who had purchasing responsibilities the power to see what would happen if they could negotiate better contracts. It gave managers the ability to see how they could profit from a more efficient process. It became a part of our culture to keep our eyes on the numbers, across the organization.

A Good Fit

In the early days of Mabel's, we worked with an accountant—and yet I was desperately trying to figure out what taxes to charge for sales in various countries. We were trailblazing in the e-commerce segment, and the easy solutions to tax collection that exist today were on a faraway horizon at that time. Manually collecting and remitting taxes from all these international sales just wasn't going to be possible. Even figuring out which ones applied to us was convoluted and complex. I had spent a considerable amount of time working on this problem and hadn't figured it out.

In an annual meeting, one of our advisors, Larry, spent time with us on our big business problems. I was describing to him my mission to crack this nut. I had laid it all out in detail, and Larry replied, "Julie, with all due respect, your accountant is not doing his job."

It was as though Larry had switched on a light bulb. I realized that although I had a responsibility to be educated and work to solutions, I shouldn't do all the research or try to figure out all the details myself. I had been feeling like an island when I should have been feeling like a well-appointed ship with a full crew to help me figure it out.

When something doesn't feel quite right, it usually isn't. When Larry flicked the switch, it forever changed how I moved forward. I knew that if it didn't feel right, I should ask questions, consult, and look for expert advice.

With trusted internal finance people in place, making sure communication lines are open between your inside team and your external accountant is critical. This ensures that information is clear and that the team is all pulling in the same direction, with the same priorities.

Be Prepared to Learn

Suffice to say, Larry introduced us to a new accountant, Bill, who met with my partners and me, took the time to understand what we really needed, and even worked with us to set our annual strategic plan. Once he understood the business and we could see the value he was able to add, moving our business to his firm was a no-brainer. The relationship with Bill lasted right up until we sold the business. In fact, without him, we couldn't have sold as quickly and with all our ducks in a row as we did. He and his team helped us put a nice bow on the deal, ensuring that we had done all we needed in order to finalize it.

Does that mean our relationship has been without bumps? Not at all. There are always bumps in the road. But we created a trusted relationship, where feedback could be given and there was open communication and discussion. This enabled a long-term partnership.

One of the strengths of this relationship was the ability of Bill and his team to teach my cofounders and me with more complexity over time, working with our in-house finance team to determine what we needed to know next as we dug into the numbers. At one point, he even helped us with a key finance hire. This added incredible value.

I encourage you to look for an accountant or financial advisor who will guide you to understand the numbers on a deeper level. This person could also be someone in your organization who works with the numbers on a daily basis and can easily interpret them for you.

That distillation of information is key—how can something complex be broken down into simple terms that everyone on the team can understand? Here are some tips.

Define the problem. Ensuring that you carefully and clearly define a problem is crucial to knowing what numbers you need. What are you trying to solve? What answer are you looking for? Have you clearly outlined the problem, and broken it down? If you're trying to save money on purchasing raw materials from your suppliers, do you know what all the various costs are so that you have a starting point? Are you looking simply for lower costs, or longer payment terms, or something else altogether? We negotiated different deals with our various suppliers (payment terms, yearly buying thresholds), looked for less expensive options to use, and sourced backup suppliers, sometimes all at the same time!

Assess the worth. Once you know what you're trying to solve for, you can dig deeper on the numbers—but is it worth it? Be careful about getting into diminishing returns. Are the extra hours, days, or weeks spent gathering the data you need, creating the delivery method, and then keeping it up to date worth the investment? Anything you dig deep on or make very complex must also be maintained. Decide how much time is worth it based on what you're likely to get out of it. Procuring many pieces of information can quickly consume much of a person's time and, frankly, may not be worth it. Every team member's time is valuable and can potentially be refocused on something much more productive to move the business ahead.

Use active listening. Asking questions for understanding is always important. Going in the wrong direction because you hesitated to ask a question or clarify a statement is always a waste of time. Even if you don't understand the numbers as deeply as others do, as the founder, you likely know the business best. Plus, your intuitive knowledge is immensely valuable. At the same time, listening carefully is vital. Active listening can help ensure understanding: try reframing what you have heard, in your own words, and speaking it back to the person delivering the information. Say something like, "So, if I understand correctly, what you are saying is..." and use your own words to explain. Then, if you have missed the mark anywhere, you'll know immediately and can ask questions to clarify.

Building Think-Big Teams

Learning any new business is a steep curve and a lot of hard work! Figuring out those mechanisms that run the business and most profoundly impact the numbers game is key. Some businesses are very complex, and it's difficult to dig down into the numbers to see what really matters. These numbers can help you decide on your vision and how you want to chase it.

Want to drive sales? Well, ramping up advertising might work, but is it the most cost-effective way? Want to cut expenses? It's easy to see where that might be possible if you have a clear picture. Understanding the numbers can also drive a culture in which continuous improvement on spending and negotiating better costs are ingrained in your workforce.

When Alyssa Kerbel of Mini Mioche wanted to take her business to the next level, she knew she would need an advisor who could help with her ideas and next-level problems. The advisor turned out to be a team of two women. One had the overall focus for the CEO, and the other helped with the financial aspects of the business. As they dug deeper into it, Alyssa found herself looking at the sales numbers for every product she sold. Colors, sizes, products—so many numbers! She quickly realized what products were profitable and which ones were not. With this data at her fingertips and learning what was core to the values she wanted to follow, she ultimately decided to simplify both her product offerings and the business itself.

Once you have the team in place and the numbers are working for you, decision-making time comes quickly behind. There are many tips and tricks to help facilitate better decisions. Let's uncover some of them.

BIG GORGEOUS TAKEAWAYS

- Selling at a loss is never sustainable and will sink your business.

- Ensure coordination between your outside advisors and your team on the inside.

- Create systems to assist you in decision making.

- Lean on the team to learn what you need.

8

THE CHOICES

How to Make Big Decisions

de·ci·sion

/dəˈsiZHən/ *noun*

a conclusion or resolution reached after consideration

FOR A LONG TIME, I found decisions tough. I didn't understand that my hesitation itself was a decision. My team would look at me with their eager eyes, waiting for direction, and I would feel pressured and a little miserable. Whether I couldn't get the support from my cofounders or my accountant for the decision I wanted to make or I was struggling to recommend an action, it was not a good scenario. I didn't feel convincing, and that frustrated me.

As the business grew and the stakes became higher, making decisions only seemed to get harder. I faced new scenarios all the time. Our homegrown software became more complex, and the team needed to run it grew. We were constantly devising and executing the next big idea to build the business, deciding that we shouldn't (or couldn't!) do things the same way anymore because we were getting too big for it to work. Plus, as my team grew, the business needs got more complex, and there were always more people relying on Mabel's Labels to support their families. It could feel like a lot of pressure and, during stressful times, inertia sometimes set in. Then, on a particularly hard day, one of my mentors told me that dragging my feet would not build my team's confidence in me. Not having considered this impact of my indecisiveness, I was taken aback.

So, I did what any ambitious entrepreneur would do: I summoned my grit and learned some hard skills for good decision making. The first lesson? Trusting your decisions begins with a clear process for making them.

The 10 Percent: Stand in Your Decisions

Thinking big means learning how to stand in your decisions. The alternative is interminably sitting in them, which is definitely not a reach-for-the-stars position.

Decision making relates to trusting yourself. We make decisions all the time—from what work to prioritize to whether to attend an event to what to have for dinner. But sometimes we get caught up in analysis paralysis. A clearly articulated decision-making process (and outlining it to your team) is hugely empowering for quick decisions and nimble, efficient forward movement.

The other thing about decisions? They need to be made. Not deciding is just as much of a choice, and it will be noticed by your team and linger in the air. Determine how to move forward to the decision point. Gain the momentum that begins with a choice.

The 90 Percent: Build Good Strategies for Decision Making

How do you decide? You probably get gut feelings about decisions. Do you listen to what your gut is telling you? We aren't always connected to what it has to say, but you can begin to build a solid foundation for your decision-making framework by tuning in to your gut when faced with a choice. There are certain techniques and signals to look out for.

The instant read. An instant read is when you meet someone or hear about a possibility and immediately respond. Intuition plays a part in this. Your gut tells you which direction to go in. Perhaps you often decide instantly, based on instinct. Can you find the business case to support it? If not, why? Does a slight hesitation signal the importance of the decision, or something more? If your decision-making framework is telling you an answer different from your gut feeling, explore that. Do you need more information? Have you missed something? Or are you just afraid to move forward? If the latter is the case, then it might be time to take the plunge!

The niggle. This is the quiet thought in the back of your head that persists. Can't sleep at night? Feel like there's something important that is just outside your reach? Listen to these signals. Look for the missing information so that it can inform your decisions.

The false lead. These are situations in which your gut steers you off course. They are often repetitive triggers. When you're under pressure to make a decision, you may not think clearly or remember your past mistakes. There is a difference between using the signals from your gut and deciding based on emotion. Often, emotion prompts you to act without the basis of facts at all. Sticking to a clearly outlined process, a few of which I talk about below, reduces emotion's influence over the decision.

A written record. I also recommend writing things down. (I always use a notebook.) In the process of deciding, take notes about everything you learn. Jot down questions about it, pieces that seem to be missing, what your gut is telling you. After you decide and time passes, your memory about your gut instincts becomes murky. If you think you're repeating bad behavior, you can review a written record later. With this information, you can also reflect on why the decision was filled with emotion, to see what is at the root of that.

Learning to trust your gut is an important piece of decision making. We aren't necessarily conditioned to listen to our bodies. The next time a decision is in front of you, make some notes about your gut feeling. Sit quietly and listen for what your gut has to tell you. Revisit those notes after the fact. What did your gut tell you? What was right or wrong about that?

Create Structured Processes

Do you have a structured decision-making process you can clearly articulate? I recommend making decisions based on data. Facts are fun! Any idea can seem fabulous, but to get to *yes!*, make sure you have hard facts to back it up. Communicate your decision-making criteria to your team members, as well, so that when they come to you for an answer, they structure their asks in a format that allows you to review the information and decide in a timely way. Your process doesn't need to be the same every time (and even if it largely is, you need some flexibility to accommodate different problems), but a few frameworks can help with decisions of all kinds.

The business case. This framework is pretty straightforward. You create a one-to-two-page document about the decision that includes statistics, research, numbers, and impacts on the business. What could go wrong and right are considerations too. Include a financial forecast and summarize it with enough exposition to explain the implications.

Ensure that you include a risk analysis. This is an important part of the process, especially when the decision raises the stakes. Your analysis should consider the risk to the business if the decision goes wrong. Is the risk financial, reputational, or something else? Capturing how it could affect your business if plans go awry is crucial to include in your business case.

Brainstorming with your team or stakeholders (or even some of your advisors) to create a list of risks and opportunities is a useful exercise. Gather for a predetermined amount of time to brainstorm—and time it so you stick to your plan. Create lists called "risks" and "opportunities." Take ideas for each list from the participants. No idea is a bad one. Once the time is up, or the lists are complete, then begin the process of working through them. Look for ideas that can be consolidated or are similar to each other. Can ideas be merged to create a better list? Is there anything that, after discussion, doesn't apply? Then, you can rank the list. Which considerations are the most important? Which ones have the biggest potential financial impact? Once you have these fleshed out, you can add them to your business case.

The scorecard method. This framework can be used when a decision is less quantifiable—for example, in determining whether a new product development idea fits with stated goals, or when hiring contractors. At Mabel's, I used this method when hiring consultants and facilitators:

* Assign three to five meaningful criteria for the role—for example: 1) a candidate who facilitated for another company similar in size and offering, 2) experience with the issues we would be dealing with at the meeting, and 3) acceptance from the management team. This list can be brainstormed with the key stakeholders to ensure alignment on the team.

- Give each candidate a score between 1 and 10 for each of the criteria.

- Add up the scores and determine the winner.

- Analyze the results. (For example, I might evaluate whether the criteria were broad enough to give me what I needed, and if the candidates seemed to fit the size of the spend.)

I would present my findings from the interviews and my scorecard results to my cofounders and ask for the approval I needed to move forward. It was an effective, neutral way to decide. It prevented us from campaigning for our "favorite" and allowed us to decide quickly and efficiently.

This technique can reduce your bias in the decision making, provided that you have allowed your stakeholder group to participate in the creation of the ranking criteria. It can also neutralize an emotional decision or one on which the key stakeholders strongly disagree. You could consider allowing all stakeholders to vote, scoring, and then evaluating what the results are saying.

Consulting with experts. Do this for a bigger or contentious decision—large financial spends to launch a new product, creating and hiring a key management role, and so on—those for which the business impact or reputational risk is greater. Gather the data and perhaps use the scorecard method outlined above, then run things by trusted advisors.

Trusted advisors for your business decisions can be immensely valuable and assuring. Remember my accountant, Bill? He often calls me first thing in the morning, and says, "Julie, I was out walking the dog last night, and I think we should..." It's so comforting to hear. Bill has a system that he is faithful to: he noodles with big strategy issues while he walks the dog. Whatever comes up, he sleeps on it and confirms whether it still looks good the next morning. Then my phone rings.

If you already have people you trust in or around the business, ask them to assist you with decisions. They may be paid advisors, mentors, board members, or a member of an organized group that you are part of. Choose people with subject-matter expertise or more experience than you (the operational coach, the retail expert, the marketing specialist). Speak with people whose opinions differ from yours for varied lenses on your situation. You may also want to work with multiple advisors for different purposes, some you meet with regularly and some you access on occasion.

Action

When is the right time to decide? Sometimes the business will inform you of timing—for example, when you have a deadline. So, you move through processes like those outlined above and decide on time.

Some decisions don't have a specific deadline. In such cases, establishing one may be of benefit, especially when a team member is waiting for approval of a recommendation or proposal so that they can proceed with their work. If you ignore or procrastinate about the decision, your employee may feel their work is not valued, and this can lead to lower engagement. All the more reason to set yourself a deadline and stick to it.

Sometimes, even after using all these methods, you find yourself still struggling. Here's what I suggest: Set some limits on your decision making. Perhaps you talk to only two or three people you trust. Not to opinion shop, but to access their expertise and honest opinions. After those conversations, give yourself twenty-four hours during which you do not seek more answers. Exercise, get fresh air and a proper amount of sleep, and generally take care of yourself. Then, decide.

Once you decide, the information must cascade down to those who need to know. Communicating the decision well is as important as making it in the first place. Sharing the business case and the decision-making tools you used creates a road map for teams as they embark on a new project. Keeping in mind the scope (so that you can evaluate project success later), as well as the anticipated risks and benefits, fosters engagement. It will also be a useful measuring stick as things unfold.

If you need buy-in from others, such as investors or business partners, schedule a meeting and present your findings. If you have done the homework, you'll be ready to present.

Decisions Gone Bad

The truth is, not all decisions are going to be right or good. To recover from a bad decision, pull the chute—and fast! Get out quickly, with as little expense as possible, and consider why the decision went wrong. Weigh out factors like reputational risk and how to exit well.

But realize, too, that if you have never made a bad decision, then you haven't made *enough* decisions. And if your decisions always appear to be "good," you're probably being too cautious. Some bold moves take nerves of steel! That's why risk analysis is important—to ensure that you and your team fully understand the stakes. It may also guide you about the right time to abort the plan, when and if that time comes.

Consider as well, though, the risk of doing nothing. Will a competitor use your lack of progress to their advantage? Or perhaps there is no risk attached to non-action. This would certainly change the urgency of that decision!

Conduct a Postmortem

When you're on the other side of a decision, in that you've executed the strategy and completed the project, do a postmortem to evaluate the success of the initiative and capture new learning. This is one way of evaluating programs, decisions, and outcomes. Gather the key stakeholders, including employees from all levels who touched the project, for a half-hour meeting to create a one-page document that captures your answers to these questions:

* What did you do really well?

* What would be even better next time if it were added to the project?

* What lessons were learned? (Choose two or three based on the points above.)

Draw from this document the next time you have a similar decision or are running a similar program.

What happens after the postmortem? You move on.

When you are working on multiple projects in different stages all at once, the cadence of good decision making will help you run the business efficiently, with stellar communication and engaged, high-performing teams.

Making Big Decisions

Women seem to be particularly good at simultaneously knowing what they want and coming up with a bunch of reasons why we should probably do something else. We often want to make nice and do the right thing. We never want to let anyone down.

Remember Kelsey Ramsden, the CEO of MINDCURE and twice-named entrepreneur of the year? When Kelsey can't decide on something, she uses a somewhat irreverent technique. "I flip a coin," she said. "When I'm in those crux moments of uncertainty, about a goal or a dream or a vision... I flip a coin... I throw the coin in the air, and there's this instant, when the coin lands, when my truest, non-ego-driven, gut self is like, 'Oh, I know the answer.' Just for a second, before my ego overrides and logic and all this other stuff come in."

Sometimes, there's just no way around a decision that takes you far outside your comfort zone. This is especially true when your business, life, or career feels like it's on shifting sand and choices feel risky.

Trivinia Barber started her business because she recognized a need in the marketplace. As an executive assistant, she kept encountering entrepreneurs who asked her to match them with an EA. So she started matchmaking and charging a small fee. That fee grew exponentially. But the decision to commit solely to her business didn't come instantly. "I like to say I'm the accidental entrepreneur, because I never set out to make a million dollars," she said. "Suddenly, my business was generating seven figures in revenue." Still, the safe base of her own EA position was seductive. "It was two years before I finally quit my day job. I was too scared, thinking, *What if this isn't real? What if it falls apart? What if it goes away?* I was so frozen by the what-ifs, so I resisted letting go of the stability. Instead, I needed to realize that I had created my own stability."

This was a paradigm shift for Trivinia—and one that happened as she learned to trust herself and her decisions.

Ultimately, knowing that your decisions are aligned with your goals can help you trust them. Shaina Azad's first vision for SUVA Beauty was broad. She wanted to produce a product for her customers that was more accessible and approachable than what was already on the market. As the business developed, so did her vision for her brand, which became much more calculated and specific. She knew that she was in a niche market, but after being in business for a couple of years, she was faced with a decision about placement in large retailers. This led to the realization that it was better for her company to stay niche—and that its niche was actually huge. Her company was best served when it was in the places that were true to her brand—that is, where her values aligned with those who were going to sell her product. This understanding allowed her to let go of the concept of the company being too small or too large. It enabled her to find a spot in the middle, which gave the brand way more traction. This turning point allowed her and her team to make the right pitches, close the right deals, and negotiate for what truly fits with their goals and plans.

BIG GORGEOUS TAKEAWAYS

- Making effective decisions with a clearly articulated process is a win for any leader.

- Analysis paralysis is a trap.

- Learning to trust yourself is an important part of decision making.

9

CARING FOR YOURSELF

How to Survive
the Roller Coaster

self-care

/ˌselfˈker/ *noun*

the practice of taking an active role in protecting one's own well-being and happiness, in particular during periods of stress

O NE SUNDAY MORNING, my husband was driving our son to sports. The kiddo was probably around ten years old. He asked my husband why traffic was so light that morning, not busy as usual. My husband replied that it was the weekend, and most people didn't have to go to work. My son was shocked—he had never considered that most people weren't like his entrepreneur parents, who worked at all kinds of odd hours.

My husband is a real estate agent, and as my business partners and I built the business at Mabel's Labels, I was fortunate that he had a flexible schedule, so we could divide the labor of raising a family and running a household. We shared responsibility for school pickups and household tasks like cleaning and groceries, as well as all the running around we did as parents of three busy children. We operated in a "high five at the front door" mentality as we handed off the family responsibilities to each other. This allowed us both to focus exclusively on our jobs when we needed to. We could also unplug from work when we were at home with the kids.

I spent many years getting up early and tackling my inbox before my children were out of bed. Then I'd put my phone and computer away and spend the time before day care or school shuttling them out the door. My husband was often out at work in the evening. Because I did my emails before everyone woke up, I could spend time with the kids after dinner.

Not everybody has such an ideal situation, but being intentional about when you work and when you step away is so important for achieving a big gorgeous goal. You've got to recharge so that you have the energy to pursue it! Finding what works for you takes time. You may also have to experiment to establish an effective system of balancing work and life.

The 10 Percent: Self-Care Is a Key Qualification for Your Role

The thing about entrepreneurship—it's a roller coaster! You are on top of the world with a win one moment and in the depths of despair with a setback the next. You feel as if you know what you're doing, and suddenly you see another mountain on the horizon, and you need to be ready for the climb. As your business grows, your level of responsibility increases; the job requires that you constantly learn. Who you are in the early days of your business is not who you need to be when you have fifty employees reporting to you and you have so many more moving parts.

Over the journey of my career, I haven't always been good at self-care. Yes, I did things like get a massage or pedicure from time to time, activities I enjoyed, but I lacked the focus on myself as a whole person. I didn't always know how to lift myself out of the doing and look at the bigger picture.

The resounding sentiment I have heard from women entrepreneurs is that they work so hard growing their business, they don't have time for "extras." Many of us categorize self-care activities as "things we know we should do"; we may even intend to do them, but somehow they always fall to the bottom of the list. But what if you considered self-care as a responsibility that comes with the job? If you nourish yourself as you go after a big gorgeous goal, you will be more likely to sustain the energy for the long game.

The 90 Percent: Care for Yourself and Your Team

Building a business is a marathon, not a sprint. Think of track-and-field athletes: the difference between a sprinter and a marathon runner is easy to spot. The sprinter has a different physique, with bulkier legs, designed for speed. The marathon runner is lean and trim, ready to run for days. And their performances are remarkably different. A sprinter explodes down or around the track in an all-out performance that takes a very short amount of time. Marathon runners set a pace they can sustain for the long haul. Pacing is important, as is keeping some gas in the tank to accelerate to the finish line.

As a leader, you need to be both a sprinter and a marathoner. Bursts of high-intensity exertion are necessary sometimes as you rush to complete a deliverable or project. But you've got to be careful about how and when you choose to sprint. Not everything is an emergency.

Most of an entrepreneur's work, though, is like a marathon. You need to set a pace you can maintain, as well as deadlines for your work that hold tension by being both realistic and a stretch to achieve. Then you need to progress. Every day. Every hour. Pacing, pacing, pacing in a rhythm for you and your team to settle into.

Do you have a good pace, or do you finish your week wondering where the time went, after working seventy hours in a blur of running from one frantic situation to another? Are you in a long-term sprint? Even if you feel great (or okay) doing this now, it's not a long-term or sustainable pace, and it has consequences for you, your business, and your team members, who likely don't see you as the Wonder Woman you think you are. They may also ask themselves whether you expect them to work the same long hours at this frantic pace.

When you set a maintainable pace, have good work-life boundaries, and take the time to restore yourself, you build resilience for the inevitable moments when you need to think creatively and keep reaching upward, outward, and in the direction of your big gorgeous goal.

Burnout

Do you separate your work life from your home life? Can you find a flow of work and life that sustains you? It may help to recognize that keeping the balance is about what works right now. Whatever you are doing right now might not work next week, next month, or next year. When it stops working, experiment until you find what does work for you in the moment.

Nowadays, finding this balance is increasingly a challenge. The ground is shifting more quickly, and knowing what will come next is difficult. The COVID-19 pandemic only underscored whatever issues we may have with separating work and life, with so many setting up a home office in the living room, a corner of the kitchen, the bedroom... That makes separating things *hard*.

In this work-from-home era, it can be especially difficult to balance work and life. But a lack of this balance is one of the many factors that contribute to burnout. In such a state, physical and emotional exhaustion may set in. You may lack a sense of accomplishment. You may even feel disconnected from your sense of personal identity. How could you chase world domination while you feel that way?

So, how do you stop yourself from getting there?

For starters, you need to maintain some boundaries between work and life. Be intentional about taking time to refresh and make sure it happens. Get outside. Do something you love and that isn't about getting to "inbox zero." Yes, there will be occasional emergencies and they will throw off your balance. That's okay—but don't make it a habit. Evaluate what constitutes an emergency and, when one comes up, tackle it. Then, as soon as you can, get back on track with your work-life limits. A friend told me that she shuts the top of her laptop with a snap when her day is done. Another closes the door to her home office when she quits for the day. Both of these actions are a physical reminder that work time is over. Setting limits will refresh you, and you'll likely find that you are more productive with them in place.

Food, Exercise, and Sleep

When you live on the run, exercising, eating well, and getting enough sleep naturally fall by the wayside. My coaching clients are often surprised when I ask them about these things, and like me, they often find that, on reflection, they have some work to do in this area. Do you eat well, exercise regularly, and sleep seven to nine hours a night? You are a whole person and, like me and my clients, if you don't have the energy to bring all of yourself to everything that you do, you will likely struggle.

Eating well. What does eating well mean? It means: please, don't eat fast food every day. Too much junk food will affect your weight, your clarity of thinking, and ultimately your ability to be there for your team and your family while you go for your big gorgeous goal.

Nourishing your body takes a bit of planning, and the investment is for the long haul. Plan to eat well-balanced meals with fresh ingredients, with a good balance of veggies (not just potatoes—eat your greens!), whole grains, and protein. Lessen how much processed food you eat. I used to batch cook on Sunday afternoons so that we had lots of meals prepped in the fridge for the busy week ahead. I loved those Sunday afternoons, as I adore being in the kitchen. From time to time, a few friends and I would cook together. We'd turn out around thirty meals between the three of us, divide them up, and fill our freezers for a couple of weeks. We also had some great laughs and conversation as we cooked. Cooking is not for everyone, though, and fortunately there are a lot of other options. Consider subscription meal plans or boxes with all the ingredients included. Or seek out preprepared food from your local grocer, health-food store, or favorite restaurant. When you eat, actually stop working and enjoy meals with yourself or your friends, family, or coworkers.

Exercise. Exercise is essential for optimal physical and mental health. Going to the gym; working out at home; or riding your bike, walking, and other physical activities can also offer time and space to think. In fact, some of the best problem solving happens while walking. With the change of scenery, try to allow your mind to wander and ponder the things you're stuck on. Or you may prefer to catch up on a favorite podcast or audiobook, or to listen to music or just the sounds around you as you move.

Spending time outdoors in nature is one way to increase your happiness as well as your fitness. I aim to spend time outdoors every day. I have also been known to do walk-and-talk meetings with my coaching clients and team. This removes us from the familiar and allows for more open thinking. Whether you are in person together or on the phone—walking in separate towns or even different countries—time spent in nature can expand everyone's thinking. Let the beauty help you welcome in new ideas or approaches.

Sleep. Why is sleep so important? In Arianna Huffington's book *The Sleep Revolution*, the author and media mogul says: "By helping us keep the world in perspective, sleep gives us a chance to refocus on the essence of who we are. And in that place of connection, it is easier for the fears and concerns of the world to drop away."

Sleep is so easy to put aside when you are busy—less sleep means you can get more things done, right? Slowly, though, you may slip into the habit of getting five hours (or even less) a night. This happens to every entrepreneur I know! That's why you need to regularly assess whether your sleep habits are meeting your needs. If they aren't, great. You are aware of it, so you can adjust. Although it may feel counterintuitive, working less to sleep more will make you more productive— that is the strange truth about getting enough sleep.

Think of it as a job requirement. For one, you need sleep to aid in decision making. Human brains need the time to rest and reset, so that they can work more efficiently. Plus, in a recent article, "Why Do We Need Sleep?," Danielle Pacheco reported that people who get more sleep are more productive and better able to process their memories, concentrate, and think clearly. The proper amount of sleep also helps your body stay healthy by fighting off viruses and other health issues.

If you are chronically short on sleep, establishing a new routine may feel arduous. Creating a ritual around bedtime can help you drift off to dreamland. Whether it's having a bath, changing into special pajamas, or putting your phone aside for an hour before bedtime, create space before bedtime to facilitate a good night's sleep. Consider leaving your phone outside your room while you sleep, as well—then you will be less tempted to check for updates if you wake in the middle of the night.

I have found that periods of difficult sleep often coincide with big challenges, problems to solve, or feeling of vulnerability. Perhaps I'm venturing into new territory—like writing my first book! These periods always pass, but they can make for some tough stretches. When I'm not sleeping well, I revert to a couple of tried-and-true methods: I turn the clock away, so I don't lie there for hours looking at it. I place a small notepad by the bed, so that if I wake up with my mind racing, I can quickly brain dump on a piece of paper and know that I won't forget any of those (potentially) great ideas.

Build resilience for the journey ahead. With a good diet, regular exercise, and sleep (every night), you can create a solid foundation on which to navigate the fires that spring up each day. And you will be in a position to step back and review, from a distance, the challenges that come.

Vacation

Another important part of refreshing your mind and body is taking a vacation. In the early days of running a business, it might feel ridiculous to even think of taking a vacation. This makes it all the more important for you to figure out how much you're going to take, schedule it, and then *go*!

Maybe you can't always get away for a full week or two. If not, be creative. Go on a day trip close to home. I live about a forty-five-minute drive from Niagara Falls. Before I committed to self-care practices like taking vacations, I used to joke that my kids had never seen the falls—but that's not true any longer. For years, though, they had never been there and had no idea that we lived so close to one of the Wonders of the World.

Here's another vacation trick: Delete your email from your phone. How scared do you feel by that suggestion? In the early days of building Mabel's Labels, I would *not* have been able to do this. But I could limit how often I checked emails while I was away. I would hop on at a couple of strategic times during the day, limit myself to twenty minutes, then close it and move on. Later, when a team reported to me, I let them know that I wouldn't be checking my email, and that they should go to a designated person in case of an emergency. That designated person was to text me if business really hit the fan.

And know, too, that this isn't just about you—it's about showing your team that you value their practices of self-care. It behooves them, you, and the business for your employees to be rested and refreshed. You won't encourage them to take time off without doing it yourself. As a founder, you are leading by example, and your team is watching how you balance work and life.

Take your vacation. Encourage your team to take theirs. The team will be more productive and happier for it.

Finding Balance in Big

Generosity will also feed your resilience. When you are generous with others, you gain. Every woman I interviewed for this book described how other women entrepreneurs and mentors have been sources of strength and resilience, because good ones will vet ideas, cry with you when things go wrong, celebrate with you when you win, and more. When you are coaching someone on how to pace themselves, you will naturally look at yourself and figure out if you are practicing what you preach; being that coach may help you stick with the slow, steady pace that you need to make it through the long haul. It keeps you accountable for setting a good example.

Alyssa Kerbel of Mini Mioche takes care of herself by doing things that bring her joy, energy, and purpose. "I look for how I can use my platform to give back in a more meaningful way," she said to me. "I want to sell kids clothes in a really sustainable and ethical way. I don't need more. I want to continue to have a great business, and I want a business that lives on and does good things. But my motivation is now to give back, which is what my business allows me to do in the world. I ask how we can serve some bigger mission through the business." For Alyssa, finding meaning in her work sustains a long-term mindset for leadership.

Kindness to yourself is an important part of self-care, too. No one gets it right all the time. I know that! I have often needed someone else to point out to me that my work-life balance was off. This can make you feel vulnerable. But self-care is an ever-changing process. What worked before may not work now. If it doesn't, step back and evaluate what will.

BIG GORGEOUS TAKEAWAYS

- Discovering and doing what restores and grounds you will fuel you over the long haul as you reach for your big goal.

- Especially when you work from home, maintaining good work-life balance is integral to navigating change.

- Proper nutrition, exercise, and rest builds resilience to withstand the inevitable stressful and busy times.

- You model self-care for your teams.

- Doing meaningful work and giving back are important aspects of self-care.

CONCLUSION

A Bigger Yes

A S WOMEN ENTREPRENEURS, we juggle so many things. Some of us are mothers. Some of us are caring for family members. Some of us are pushing hard against societal barriers. And so much more. These roles affect us deeply. Sometimes, taking care of it all *and* achieving a big goal feels overwhelming. Sometimes, we accomplish that great thing and then, having reached the summit, realize it was only a plateau. Now we need to summon our energy and wits to set a new goal and begin the climb yet again.

When I became a coach, I knew I needed to step into my dreams. I wanted to build a dynamic business with a base of entrepreneurs and executive clients who would reach their fullest potential through our work together; I wanted to deliver life- and career-changing workshops and deliver keynote speeches that audiences would feel illumined and inspired by. And those ambitions led me to writing this book.

Once I had defined those goals and put them out in the world, I needed to get to work manifesting them, even though I felt afraid and uncertain. I had to sit down at the table where the jigsaw puzzle of my life and career was laid out for me and arrange the pieces. I needed to do the big, strategic thinking that I had done so many times before for Mabel's and our team—only this time, I needed to do it for myself.

You, too, are capable of setting a big gorgeous goal and reaching for the stars. This certainly isn't the easiest path to take. But when you decide to go for world domination, with ambition so big it blocks out the sun, a particular energy enters the room, and it makes you want to expand. When you move through whatever stops you from pursuing your big goal and say yes, you enter the land of abundance. Your best self lives there—where you feel creative and whole, emotionally, spiritually, and intellectually. Saying a bigger yes is part of that path.

The point is to live up to your full potential.

Look for the wonder and excitement as you pursue your big gorgeous goal, as you stretch outside your comfort zone. It can be a scary place, so finding fun and excitement is key to staying motivated. Surround yourself with other big thinkers on their own paths—supporting one another makes the journey more enjoyable and success easier to imagine.

I challenge you to reflect on a think-big mindset. Set a big gorgeous goal. And say a bigger yes!

Saying a Bigger Yes

All the women I interviewed for this book have encountered challenges, and yet they continually say a bigger yes to their gorgeous goals. As you set your own big gorgeous goal and go after it, here are some words of wisdom you can keep in mind from other women on the journey, carving the path with you.

Ask for help. Vicki Saunders of SheEO has done a massive amount of work to decondition herself over the years, taking her vision from one of scarcity to one of abundance. Now, one of her base assumptions is that there will be enough to go around. Vicki told me:

> I really believe this is one of the most fundamental lies that blocks us from being who we can be: as women, we are always telling ourselves to do it on our own or to be perfect before we go anywhere. This leads to isolation and not asking for help and staying small. We keep it small because it's just so hard to go bigger. I never knew what we could realize by just asking for help. It's a gift. This constant cycle of giving, receiving, and reciprocating changes everything. It's a whole different world, and walking through the door from the old world has made me realize that you are usually only one step removed from whatever you need.

Plan for the plateau. You might be able to keep your momentum during a time of big change by planning for the plateau that you know will come. About four or five years before Tammy Barlette retired from the US Air Force and started her women veteran speakers' company, she knew she needed a plan.

> I realized over the next few years that if I retired and didn't do anything else, it would mean the twenty years I spent doing this was a bit of a waste. I decided I needed to give back. I heard many women saying, "I can't be a fighter pilot because I want to have kids." Or that they didn't see women doing it. [I realized that] if I did what a lot of women do—retire, hide, because I didn't want to be egotistical or to have people looking at me ... the ones behind us wouldn't see us go before them, and then the path would need to be paved over and over again.

My goal is to shine a light on the path. So anyone behind me can get further than I got. This led me to start Athena's Voice, because I knew I wasn't going to be flying forever. They need a lot more of us women fighter pilots out there. One of our audiences is women: we have a real impact on this category. So, Athena's Voice was born. We recruited other chick fighter pilots that we knew and went from there.

Show up for yourself. BE Alink follows her North Star. Big thinking led BE to start her company, Alinker Inventions, and she is always looking forward to the next and bigger thing. She said:

We are supposed to experience life in a certain way and behave in a certain way. Instead, I have turned away. I look at how I want to live and how I want to show up for people. How I want to show up for myself. We are conditioned to identify problems and go fix them—that is what serves the system. Perceived problems are often just symptoms of systems that are not designed for our well-being, so I don't engage; I turn around and imagine what is possible, without the constructs of the perceived problems.

"It's about taking my expertise and what I'm good at," Julie Kenney, CEO of Jewels and Pinstripes, told me. "I like big ideas, and I love building relationships. When you are part of a business for a long time, you need to see yourself outside of that light and how much you have to give. You realize that you've done so many things—you can take that and use it to lever yourself forward."

Go for freedom. Mini Mioche's Alyssa Kerbel told me, "My big goals now are to feel good and to have balance. I can work from anywhere and create my own schedule. I have all the things entrepreneurs really want but have a really hard time achieving when they first set out on this journey. I can see now that it's possible."

Own your ambition. Janet Kestin, one of Swim's two cofounders, touched on how important it is to overcome the idea that we should stay small. She said,

> I was on a trip in Italy with a group of women. Each night, we had a table topic to discuss. One topic that came up was ambition. We were all in very good jobs, but every one of us was unbelievably uncomfortable with the word "ambition." We wanted to go after things. We had goals and dreams. We had already achieved. But to ally ourselves with that word, with that idea, felt against what we were raised to think of as acceptable for women. We talked and talked about it. And one year later, every one of us had a giant career leap.

Janet's partner in Swim, Nancy Vonk, added, "Now we have transitioned into a second career all about helping others excel as leaders, which is ironic considering how long we didn't consider ourselves as leaders. We did that for years, not recognizing what leadership is. Doing it our way was a big part of saying yes."

Stretch yourself. Fotini Iconomopoulos, founder of Forward Focusing, surrounds herself with interesting people who have fascinating ideas. She said, "When you surround yourself with the cream of the crop, and you realize that there are lots of ways to keep stretching yourself—that's where I find new goals, and that is what opportunity looks like. Then you can say yes to that."

Rely on yourself. Kelsey Ramsden of MINDCURE touched on how often entrepreneurs must rely on their own wits to figure things out for themselves. "You have to keep the dream and the vision and pursue them," she said. "When we are innovating and leading, there isn't a way it has been done. There isn't some-one else to look to, and that's uncomfortable. So much of it is intuitive for me. I see this thing, and I rally my team toward it."

Make those changes. Diana Bishop was at the very top of her career. She knew she wasn't going to go higher, and she wanted to do something else. She was terrified and needed to find a way to ease herself into something new. She started telling her own stories through documentaries. After she left news-casting for good, she founded her business, The Success Story Program, to help politicians, business leaders, and entrepre-neurs tell their stories.

Engage your values. Sandy Stosz, retired vice admiral in the US Coast Guard, spoke to how the best decisions about the direction of a career or business are driven by a woman's own values and what will fulfill them. Sandy said:

> I am a firm believer that people who make it to the top have personal core values they don't divert from and work hard to stay true to that North Star. They can't be pulled into doing something unethical. They can't quit because they get overwhelmed or are unsure of themselves. So,

they must have a core value set that keeps them on a straight and narrow course. They have to reach out for other people to ally with them. They must be willing to do the hard work and to persevere. But also to take the small steps. Find the motivation to want to work hard, to keep pursuing the next level up, but realize it's a journey, not just getting to the destination.

Acknowledge your people. Shaina Azad's family is incredibly supportive of her big dreams for SUVA Beauty, and as a power-house woman business owner, she strives to be an exceptional role model for her kids. Her eldest son told her, "I have a little suitcase in my pocket, and I'm going to go to the office and take over the world like Mommy."

When angel investor Karen Grant thinks of all the really big things she has done, she appreciates that she didn't do them alone: "I have been fortunate with the people who have lent a hand and helped me along." For Karen, this is the enduring theme of the network she has cultivated, as people return to her with opportunities over and over again.

"Looking at the whole ecosystem—that's the way I think," Lori Weir of Four Eyes Financial told me. She spoke of how the people around her influence her approach to expansive think-ing. "I don't think about a quick fix to a single problem but about the bigger picture. I like to surround myself with like-minded people, and this has been very key for having the confidence to move forward, toward where I think the end goal will be."

Paula White of Side B Consulting said, "I love to build, then let go and move on to build something else. It's delightful to sit back and look at all the opportunities you have created for yourself and others."

It's good to chill out. Executive-assistant-turned-entrepreneur Trivinia Barber said, "Chasing big goals has been a journey. It has not been easy. I have learned that leading means constantly growing as a human, as those goalposts move out and the company grows. I have had to learn to pause and celebrate where we have come [from], not just look at the next goalpost we want to reach. I want to sit here for a bit and celebrate—do a happy dance."

Public relations maven GG Benitez needs to remind herself that it's okay to chill out sometimes too! "I haven't fully figured it out yet, but I am trying to tell myself that," she said. "I love to hustle and make things happen. Those habits create a path toward success. I am a person of my word, and I always follow through."

Go Big!

You have a unique reason for going after your next big gorgeous goal. Whatever your background or motivations, I'm willing to bet that what you want to accomplish isn't boring or expected. Your ambitions are awe-inspiring, so much so that they may even spark fear in you. But what sizeable goal isn't worthy of a little quaking in your boots? I'm also willing to bet your goal is something the world wants and needs. You are an entrepreneur, after all. Your very business has formed, or is forming, to solve a problem you identified. You knew you could improve the situation.

My wish for you is that you chase your big gorgeous goal with joy and balance—and a hefty dose of grit. You know by now that you're going to need it! I hope you find people who will pick you up when you fall and help you get there. I never imagined I could do the things I have accomplished, and I know that you can do your things as well. Set that big gorgeous goal. Reach for the stars. And maybe you'll land on the moon. What will happen then?

ACKNOWLEDGMENTS

PROCRASTINATED IN WRITING these acknowledgments because it's impossible to thank everyone who believed in me and made this book possible.

When I first had the idea that I might write a book, it was late 2019, and I had just completed public-speaking training with Heroic Public Speaking. Amy and Michael Port opened my eyes to what building a keynote around my ideas might look like, and I quickly signed up to continue my journey at HPS.

That fall, I also joined a great book writing group, which was led by Helen Wilkie, and our biweekly gatherings and content-sharing were invaluable to the progress of my ideas. Alexandra Bohnet, Patti Pokorchak, Michelle Ray, and Helen: your advice, input, and feedback was invaluable to this book making it across the line.

Through my HPS experience, I met AJ Harper and, in fall 2020, joined her daily writing group. This group helped me get the words on the page, and I wouldn't have finished the book without the wise counsel of Laura Stone, AJ, and the various group members whose faces I enjoy seeing as I start my mornings. I wouldn't trade you for anything!

Big thanks to Liane Davey for introducing me to Trena White. It was the beginning of believing that I could actually write this! Trena and the Page Two team have been amazing to work with. I'm grateful for my editor, Kendra Ward: Kendra, without your shaping, this book wouldn't be where it is. I am so delighted to have worked with you.

To all the women I interviewed: you inspire me, you lift me up, and I admire all of you. Thanks to Diana Bishop, Fotini Iconomopoulos, Julie Kenney, Sandy Stosz, GG Benitez, Alyssa Kerbel, Lori Weir, Jalyn Anderson, Karen Grant, Paula White, Tammy Barlette, Shaina Azad, Vicki Saunders, BE Alink, Janet Kestin, Nancy Vonk, Trivinia Barber, Kelsey Ramsden, and Lisa Pellegrino.

To my privy council: thanks for always believing in me and seeing what's possible. Kelsey Ramsden, Tonia Jahshan, Tricia Mumby, Lara Dewar, and Jackie Dinsmore: I love you all, and I'm so glad you're in my life.

To my speaking gang—Jennifer Fondrevay, Paula White, Sharon Preszler, Kris Kelso, Nicole Mahoney, and Carole Stizza—thank you for all your advice and encouragement. I hope we can actually meet each other in person soon!

Thanks to my friend Shardie Stevenson: coffees and wine and chats on my porch helped me keep moving this along, and your edits and time are greatly appreciated.

To my eye-for-design friend Kate Longridge, I thank you for knowing when to print my cover designs, who to ask for feedback, and how to decide what worked best.

To the Mabel's cofounders. I couldn't and wouldn't be here without you. It has been a treat and such a fun ride. Thanks, Julie Cole, Cynthia Esp, and Tricia Mumby for thirteen *amazing* years together. Look what we did!

To my family—Dave, Katie, Owen, and Liam: thanks for putting up with me during this process, and always. Love you.

NOTES

Chapter 3
Big Gorgeous Goals: What Happens When You Reach for the Stars

When it comes to leadership qualities: See, for example: Jack Zenger and Joseph Folkman, "Research: Women Score Higher Than Men in Most Leadership Skills," *Harvard Business Review*, June 25, 2019, hbr.org/2019/06/research-women-score-higher-than-men-in-most-leadership-skills.

Research reported by Mark Murphy: Mark Murphy, "Neuroscience Explains Why You Need to Write Down Your Goals If You Actually Want to Achieve Them," *Forbes*, April 15, 2018, forbes.com/sites/markmurphy/2018/04/15/neuroscience-explains-why-you-need-to-write-down-your-goals-if-you-actually-want-to-achieve-them.

Chapter 9
Caring for Yourself: How to Survive the Roller Coaster

By helping us keep the world in perspective: Arianna Huffington, *The Sleep Revolution: Transforming Your Life, One Night at a Time* (New York: Harmony Books, 2016), 283.

people who get more sleep are more productive: Danielle Pacheco, "Why Do We Need Sleep?" Sleep Foundation, updated November 30, 2021, sleepfoundation.org/how-sleep-works/why-do-we-need-sleep.

ABOUT THE AUTHOR

JULIE ELLIS IS an executive coach to corporate leaders and scaling entrepreneurs. Her unique experience and expertise stems from twenty-five years of working first in the corporate world and then as a leading Canadian entrepreneur. She is a cofounder of the award-winning company Mabel's Labels, one of Canada's greatest small-business success stories.

Since starting her own coaching company, Julie Ellis & Co., in 2016, Julie has become a sought-after speaker and trainer, and has developed keynotes and workshops for private companies, corporations, and associations. She has motivated her audiences to "Ignite, Scale, and Exit," discover "Success Secrets of Wonder Women!," and achieve "Big Gorgeous Goals."

As a professionally certified coach with the International Coaching Federation (2020), Julie works directly with bold leaders, propelling them to unlock their capacity and leading them to accelerated success.

Julie was enlisted as the growth mentor for female-founded companies in Beyond Boundaries, a program run by Haltech and funded by the Canadian government in their efforts to double the number of women-owned businesses in Canada by 2025. She also spent eighteen months as chief operating officer for Snuggle Bugz, a privately owned omni-channel retailer based in Burlington, Ontario. She has been advising entrepreneurs through the Hamilton-based Innovation Factory and Halton-based Haltech since 2019. Julie is also chair of the board at Angel One Network, one of the most active angel investor groups in Canada.

biggorgeousgoals.com

Bring Big Gorgeous Goals to Your Organization

Now that you know you need to set some big gorgeous goals, how can you do that?

Here are four ways to get started.

Copies for Your TEAM
Buy copies for your team, and after they read the book, I will send you a presentation to use for your discussion with them.

Copies for Your ORGANIZATION
If you want to buy books for everyone, I'd love to help! Contact me to chat about bulk discounts and special offers. We can even customize or co-brand the book for your organization.

Speaking at an EVENT
If you're having an event, I'm happy to present the "Big Gorgeous Goals" keynote to get your team excited and engaged. This is a great step on the path to letting those goals live and breathe!

Workshops for the TEAM or LEADERS
Do your team members or your leaders need help uncovering those big gorgeous goals? I can help, and I'd love to come on board for either an hour or a whole day, virtually or in person.

Get Started Now

Reach out via email or the web links below, and we can talk about the options that fit you best. Looking forward to hearing from you!

- ⊕ biggorgeousgoals.com
- ✉ julie@julieellisandco.com
- ⊚ @thejulieellis
- 🔗 linkedin.com/in/julie-ellis